PALEO TAKES 5 -OR- FEWER

HEALTHY EATING WAS NEVER EASIER WITH THESE DELICIOUS 3, 4 AND 5 INGREDIENT RECIPES

CINDY SEXTON

FOUNDER OF PALEODISH

FOREWORD BY ROBB WOLF

AUTHOR OF THE *NEW YORK TIMES* BESTSELLER, *THE PALEO SOLUTION*

WITH CONTRIBUTIONS BY MATHIEU LALONDE

PAGE STREET
PUBLISHING CO.

PAGE STREET
PUBLISHING CO.

First published in 2014 by
Page Street Publishing Co.
27 Congress Street, Suite 103
Salem, MA   01970
www.pagestreetpublishing.com

Distributed by Macmillan; sales in Canada by The Canadian Manda Group; distribution in Canada by The Jaguar Book Group.

17   16   15   14   1   2   3   4   5

ISBN-13: 978-1-62414-075-4
ISBN-10: 1-62414-075-0

Library of Congress Control Number: 2014935115

Cover and book design by Page Street Publishing Co.
Photography by Ken Goodman

Printed and bound in China

Page Street is proud to be a member of 1% for the Planet. Members donate one percent of their sales to one or more of the over 1,500 environmental and sustainability charities across the globe who participate in this program.

IN MEMORY

In memory of my mom: the woman who gave me the strength to change my life. Love you always.

DEDICATION

Dearest Dustin: I am so thankful for everything you do for me day in and day out. Nothing goes unnoticed. You are my biggest supporter and I couldn't have done this project without your calming influence, skills in the kitchen and little pep talks. My rock, I love you to bits.

CONTENTS

FOREWORD | 7
INTRODUCTION | 8

 INGREDIENTS | 108

DIPS, DRESSINGS AND DRIZZLES | 192

INGREDIENTS | 20

INGREDIENTS | 52

RESOURCES | 208

VITAMINS IN FOOD | 211
MINERALS IN FOOD | 214
ACKNOWLEDGMENTS | 217
ABOUT THE AUTHOR | 218
INDEX | 219

FOREWORD

Well, hello, folks. Robb Wolf here. Cindy Sexton, aka my pal to the North, has been a gal who has been interested and involved in this Paleo movement from the early days. Our connection goes way back to the early times of my nutrition seminars. We first met back in 2009, when I came up to Canada to do a gig in Toronto, but it wasn't until time upon time after that we actually became more acquainted. Through mutual friends like Julie and Charles Mayfield and Mathieu Lalonde (The Kraken), I have had the chance to hang with both Cindy and her husband Dustin during shin-digs and over several meals and dining experiences.

I can talk with Cindy for less than a few minutes and know right away that her passion for health and wellness is strong. When she gets going she just beams. What I adore about Cindy's approach is this: It is simple, yet effective. Minimal, yet interesting. Nutrient focused, yet delicious. She doesn't overthink things and basically just goes with the flow. Her style is far from uptight—much like mine—and that is what I like. Eating well doesn't have to be so complicated.

This book is proof, case and point, that you do not need a lengthy list of ingredients to create recipes that are satisfying and wonderfully healthful. Cindy showcases her talents in this book with food ideas that will awaken your senses and leave you wondering why you were ever making it harder than it actually needed to be. With complementary pairings, Cindy's dishes pack loads of flavor by making use of fresh, nutrient dense foods. She effortlessly turns them into super yummy grub. She makes use of good fats, quality animal sources, vegetables, some fruits, nuts, seeds, herbs and spices. It really can be that easy.

When writing this book, Cindy partnered up with Mat Lalonde to make the recipes even more enlightening by highlighting certain foods and what they can bring to your plate in terms of their vitamin and mineral content. As an added bonus, Cindy's writing style will make you feel like you are right there cooking alongside her in the kitchen. A unique spin on your everyday cookbook, this one will help you to determine some of the most nutrient dense foods possible and how to include them in your repertoire.

Breakfast, lunch, dinner, whenever o'clock, this book is a breathtaking resource that gives you solutions to that age-old question of, "What do you want to eat?"

—Robb Wolf

Robb Wolf is a former biochemist and the *New York Times* bestselling author of *The Paleo Solution—The Original Human Diet*

INTRODUCTION

THE WHO?
(NO, SILLY. I DON'T MEAN THE ENGLISH ROCK BAND!)

INTRODUCING MOI

"Hi. Are you Paleo?" It's a question I get all the time. "No actually, I'm Cindy, nice to meet you!" Paleo doesn't define me, but this will help. I am a woman, daughter, sister, aunt, wife, friend and teacher. More recently I am a nutrition enthusiast, exercise girl, home cook, blogger and now...author!

But in reality, really, I am just a gal—a gal who has transformed her life completely with food and lifestyle changes. Plain and simple. I am just a gal who went from pretty much not cooking a darn thing to falling in love with chefing things up in the kitchen.

THE CATALYST

What a life-changing journey these past several years (decade+) have been! Wow! I can't believe it has been that long. What a ride.

In March 2003, my world was shaken by the sudden death of my dear mom. She was a nurturing and generous person, someone who always put others first. Unfortunately, she was diagnosed with diabetes in her thirties and she became insulin dependent. As time went on she also developed other related conditions. At the age of just 56, she suffered a massive heart attack and left our world far too soon.

Living through this has been heartbreaking. After taking time to grieve and deal with this loss, I realized that I had to reevaluate my own life, including my food choices, level of physical activity and personal goals. These were all areas that I thought I was in control of, but in reality I was overweight and sedentary. I learned from my mom's death that I had to turn my life around and take the reins of my own fate. When I was finally able to gain my ground, I was infused with strength I didn't even know I had! Sure, there have been ups and downs, but I found the motivation to get back on track. Not a day goes by that I don't think of my wonderful mom. I thank her for giving me the determination and the focus to embark on a new lifestyle.

By drastically changing my eating habits, exercise regime, sleep patterns and overall outlook on life, I have witnessed astonishing results. Not just in the way I look, but more importantly in my performance, mood and function. I am seventy(ish) pounds lighter, a heck of a lot happier and much, much stronger! I wake up with a channeled energy. I feel that I have a heightened sense of purpose and passion for what I believe in. I am thriving.

In February 2009, I reconnected with a close friend, Tyler Touchette. As my road towards greater health continued, the timing couldn't have been more perfect. Tyler, as well as countless others, has been and still is a major player in my (lifestyle) change, in bringing me to where I presently am. During our conversation at that time, he told me all about the paleo lifestyle and the strength and conditioning program/weightlifting he was involved with. Without hesitation, I decided to join the CrossFit Toronto gym in our neighborhood.

It has now been over 5 years since my husband and I experienced those "deer caught in headlights" days in the boot camp. Every day I become more and more in love with this way of life. My passion for cooking and eating "really real food" has grown remarkably. I never realized that making a few changes could make such a huge difference. This journey is far from over, and perhaps is only just beginning. I hope to continue to bloom and, in the meantime, to share some delicious recipes and tips along the way. Life is precious, live it! Here's to a healthier and fitter you. Go and love food (again)!

'REAL FOOD'

When I finished my degree at university, I moved to Toronto to start teachers college. Shortly after doing so, I met Dustin, my husband, and we moved in together. About a year later, in March of 2003, I lost my mom to a massive heart attack. This is what I call the catalyst. This was the incentive; this was the spur that I needed to start making change. However, I had to experience a dark place before this was possible. It was a bit of a roller coaster before coming to terms with everything and realizing that major adjustments were needed.

After my mom's passing, my anxiety worsened, and I started to experience full-blown panic attacks. During this time, I also injured my neck really badly and had difficulty with much exercise of any kind. Dizzy, puffy (as I call it looking back in photos), depressed and down-and-out, I went to the doctor. Guess what? He quickly prescribed medication to "help" with the anxiety, but things actually got worse for me. The side effects weren't worth it, so I weaned myself off.

Another plan was needed. In 2005, Dustin proposed to me. We started preparation for our wedding, which was scheduled for the summer of 2007. The celebration of this happy time was just what I needed to get out of this black hole. I began the Weight Watchers program. With that, I experienced much success with losing weight, but I also gained the attribute of becoming overly concerned with the scale. I was constantly counting, weighing and calculating. During this time, I thought I was eating real food, but was I really?

No. Hardly. Low-fat this, and reduced-fat that. So called heart-healthy this, all the way back to reduced-calorie that. I combed the grocery store shelves and filled our cart with 100-calorie snack packs of who knows what (actually counting their points with my calculator as I shopped), microwave dinners, pre-boxed items and bags, all of which carried glowing health claims on their packaging. The outside was made to look good, but most of what was inside was just a distant cousin of the food it declared it was. From a physical standpoint, I had lost weight, but I still wasn't healthy. My digestive issues were at an all-time high. I was definitely wearing the rose-colored glasses, and I was completely mesmerized by what the media was telling me healthy was supposed to be. I was under their spell and believed all the hype and hoopla. This up and down diet wasn't sustainable for me. It truly wasn't a lifestyle; it was a numbers game of empty calories in and calories out that I no longer wanted to be a part of. I didn't know what to do. I think many of you can probably relate, as this is where most people find themselves stuck. (Even though you might not realize it at the time).

REALLY REAL FOOD

The years following 2009, until the present, is when the true magic happened. Upon meeting up with Tyler Touchette, going to several nutrition workshops led by Robb Wolf and Mathieu Lalonde, attending numerous Ancestral Health Symposiums, it started to become clear to me. The waters became less cloudy. The haze was lifting and I was learning what I needed to do to actually become healthy. In its simplest form, I needed to eat what I now call 'really real food'.

The benefits started rolling in when I cleared out all the refined and highly processed junk, grains and legumes and replaced them with really real whole foods. I ditched the restrictive counting mentality and started to concentrate more on nourishing my body with healthful foods. I began a reciprocal relationship with food where I started to pay attention to where it came from and what it actually was. In return it started to show me some love back.

When I did so, it was life changing. Literally, I call it miraculous—digestive issues: adios; skin: much clearer; hair: shinier; anxiety: no longer; panic attacks: bye-bye; inflammation: farewell; mood swings: cheerio; sleep: like a baby; energy: hello there! I was out from hiding underneath that umbrella of what and how I thought I was supposed to feel. I was actually feeling like everyone deserves to feel—how we are meant to feel both physically and, more importantly, mentally.

THE WHAT?

BRING BACK COMMON SENSE

We live in a society where many folks want better: they want success, they want more and they want it now. The world is addicted to instant gratification; ignoring problems and fixing things with pills, detoxes, crazes, infomercials, gimmicks, magic potions and dynamic devices that have taken over. It has become a reality for some and somewhere along the line that good ol' thing called common sense has gotten all mixed up in this jumble. It's time to unscramble things a little and bring back the simplicity of home-cooked healthy meals as a way of healing.

A WORD FROM MATHIEU LALONDE PHD – WHAT IS NUTRIENT DENSITY?

Public health authorities are pleading with us to eat fewer empty calories and more nutrient dense foods. But what is nutrient density? And which foods are nutrient dense? The answer to the first question is both simple and complex. A density is, by definition, a quantity divided by a volume. So nutrient density must be the amount of nutrients in a volume of food. Now for the complications: (1) The food we eat contains a lot of different nutrients, which ones do we choose? (2) The volume of food is rarely measured, except for liquids, so what other universal variable do we pick? These last two points are the reason why scientists have yet to agree upon a definition of nutrient density.

Some grocery stores display nutrition scores in an attempt to inform their customers of a food's potential health benefits. Unfortunately, these nutrition scoring systems are not necessarily a measure of nutrient density and are clearly developed with a biased agenda in mind. Researchers have recently proposed excellent models for assessing nutrient density. The simplest and most effective states that nutrient density is the sum of all essential nutrients, divided by their respective RDA, in a standard serving of food (this can be 100 grams or more). This method yields a result that might not be too surprising to you; the most nutrient dense foods are unprocessed, whole foods like meat (beef, poultry, pork, game, fish and seafood, etc.), vegetables, nuts and seeds, herbs, spices and fruit.

But wait! We're told to consume grains, especially whole grains, because they are nutritious. Why aren't they on the list? Good question! It turns out that raw grains are reasonably nutritious but they are also inedible. Ever tried to eat a raw wheat berry? Didn't think so. Grains have to be cooked before they can be eaten and they lose a substantial amount of nutrients during the cooking process. The same is true for most legumes. That is why this cookbook focuses on the more nutrient dense meats, fish, seafood, vegetables, nuts and seeds, herbs, spices and fruit. We've highlighted the RDA of essential nutrients used in the recipes so you can see for yourself how nutritious this way of eating can be.

WITH A LITTLE HELP (WELL, MAYBE MORE THAN A LITTLE)

Throughout the process of creating this cookbook, I received some assistance from Mathieu regarding the nutrient density numbers of certain foods. We highlighted good to excellent sources of essential nutrients (vitamins and minerals) for the ingredients of most recipes. The fraction of the RDA of each essential nutrient is based on a 100 g serving of the food.

The three different descriptors that you find throughout the recipes, highlighting the nutrient density of certain foods, are "excellent," "very good," and "good." The meaning of each is as follows and is classified accordingly. Each vitamin and mineral is described according to the value ranges below.

EXCELLENT: 0.75 x RDA or greater

VERY GOOD: 0.50 to 0.74 x RDA

GOOD: 0.25 to 0.49 x RDA

If you want to take a further peek at all of this, I have included it in a chart format in the appendix at the back of the book. Now ... now, don't be alarmed or get your knickers in a knot if you turn to your favorite food and see many shaded boxes in that row. For example, if you see that there is no value written under copper, it doesn't mean that it is completely void of that mineral. It just means that it contains 10% or less of the RDA. Below you will find the vitamins and minerals that we included. As you read through the recipes, take note of the Nutrient Density Facts that we have provided at the bottom of the pages. Please note: not all foods were examined as we tried to avoid repetition and some were not available in the USDA database.

NUTRIENT-DENSITY CHART

VITAMINS	BIOCHEMICAL FUNCTION
VITAMIN A	+ Vision & the health of your skin + Immune function, cell growth, reproductive health & gene regulation + Fetal development, absorption of minerals & bone growth
VITAMIN B_p (CHOLINE)	+ Brain & liver health + Cell membrane structure & nerve communication + Development of fetus & infants + Metabolic health & reduction of inflammation
VITAMIN B_1 (THIAMINE)	+ Nervous system health/signaling + Muscle & tissue growth + Energy production + Heart health
VITAMIN B_2 (RIBOFLAVIN)	+ Energy production + Regeneration of glutathione + Vision & the health of your skin + Red blood cell production & digestive tract health
VITAMIN B_3 (NIACIN)	+ Nervous system & health of your skin/tissues + Energy production & circulation + Enzyme function/digestion + Heart, brain & pancreatic health
VITAMIN B_5 (PANTOTHENIC ACID)	+ Nervous system, brain & health of your skin + Wound health & fights infection + Energy production & adrenal support + Production of red blood cells
VITAMIN B_6 (PYRIDOXINE)	+ Nervous system, brain & the health of your skin + Production of red blood cells/oxygen in blood + Metabolism of carbohydrates + Liver detoxification & gene expression
VITAMIN B_9 (FOLATE)	+ Production & maintenance of cells and DNA + Production of red blood cells & transportation + Especially important during pregnancy/infancy

VITAMIN B$_{12}$	+ Blood cell & DNA health
	+ Brain & nervous system health
	+ Especially important for children
VITAMIN C	+ Bone & heart health
	+ Brain & cell/tissue health & repair
	+ Immune function & disease prevention
	+ Growth & development
	+ Antioxidant/pro-oxidant
VITAMIN D	+ Bone health
	+ Cell growth & development
	+ Mental health
	+ Heart health
VITAMIN E	+ Antioxidant function & skin health
	+ Gene expression
	+ Neurological health
	+ Cellular & immune health
VITAMIN K	+ Bone health
	+ Heart and kidney health
	+ Normal blood clotting

MINERALS	BIOCHEMICAL FUNCTION
CALCIUM	+ Bone & tooth health
	+ Cellular health
	+ Nervous system health
	+ Heart health
	+ Muscle contraction & blood clotting
COPPER	+ Organ function & nerve health
	+ Bone, brain & heart health
	+ Production of red blood cells
	+ Immune function, tissue repair & healthy hair
IRON	+ Production of red blood cells & enzymes
	+ Neurological function
	+ Cellular function/growth & immune health
	+ Transportation of oxygen & production of energy

MAGNESIUM	+ Growth & maintenance of cells
	+ Nervous system, bone & tooth health
	+ Energy production & metabolic function
	+ Muscle relaxation
MANGANESE	+ Bone and skin health
	+ Wound healing & cell health
	+ Blood sugar control
PHOSPHORUS	+ Tissue and cell health
	+ Energy production & pH regulation
	+ Bone & tooth health
	+ Formation of DNA
POTASSIUM	+ Managing fluids within the body
	+ Maintaining electrolyte balance
	+ Heart & cell health
	+ Nerve impulse & muscle contraction
SELENIUM	+ Thyroid health & hormone regulation
	+ Cell maintenance
	+ Brain health
	+ Digestive & autoimmune health
	+ Male prostate health
ZINC	+ Immune health
	+ Growth & development/bone formation
	+ Cell & thyroid health
	+ Skin, hair, nails & vision health
	+ Fertility & reproductive health

THE WHY?

People often ask, "Why should I start eating this way?" I say, "Why not?" I have never been one to try to personally convince or pressure anyone into anything of the sort. But the truth of the matter is, I do think eating this way is beneficial for many. I like to echo Robb Wolf's mantra of, "give it a try for 30 days, and see how you look, feel and perform." Chances are you will end up feeling a million times better and if not, then you can go back to your old ways. Easy, right? Not always, but I encourage you to give it a go.

Your project is YOU! Start making you a priority, because you matter. Your health matters. Caring for yourself is often seen as selfish but, guess what, that couldn't be further from the truth. Self care is actually selfless. It works to transform you into a better partner, spouse, parent, grandparent, employee, etc. By doing so, you're able to give yourself to others in ways that are more meaningful and productive. When I started to concentrate on bettering myself, and not worrying about the Joneses, good things started to happen.

In all seriousness though, beneath all the cutesy "caveman" stuff that is so commonly seen, there is actual science—you know, studies and stuff. There are real studies that focus on causation and not just correlation—studies that are legit and not just funded by companies and organizations that have biased agendas on producing skewed results. Check out this site, as well as the additional science section in my resources at the back, to dig a little deeper:

www.ncbi.nlm.nih.gov/pubmed

HOW CAN THIS HELP ME HEAL?

By focusing on eating really real, nutrient dense foods, you can begin to heal your body from the inside out. The microbiota of your gut has an influence on so much—your whole entire body to be exact. By focusing on repairing your gut, you find the solution to many other conditions, illnesses and diseases.

I would recommend seeking out a health practitioner who is a functional medicine doctor that will guide and help you achieve health along the way. This partnership could be the answer to putting an autoimmune condition into remission, balancing your hormones, losing weight, reversing diabetes, Alzheimer's, Parkinsons, multiple sclerosis, certain cancers, autism, ADHD, heart disease and restoring your mental health. The list goes on and on. The truth is that many conditions are treatable, reversible and perhaps even preventable in the first place when adapting a paleo lifestyle. Locate a trained medical professional through the links below that can help you on your way!

www.paleophysiciansnetwork.com
www.primaldocs.com

IT TAKES TIME

Making change and waiting for results to happen takes time. Remember, it isn't a quick fix. My challenge to you is to sit back, relax and enjoy the ride. Celebrate your small accomplishments, as those are what can lead to bigger ones. Don't dwell if you choose to indulge. Go with the flow, chill and learn to have fun cooking in the kitchen. Stressing out doesn't do a body good! Put the 'snowball effect' into full force here! (In a good way).

TWEAK AS YOU GO

What works for one person may not work for another. Context matters as each individual person may be coming at the change from a different point. Experiment, tweak and alter things as you go. Don't get caught in being dogmatic about certain foods, but just pay attention to how your body is responding and reacting. Remember watching Bob Ross on television paint at his easel? You need to take his advice and create what you will. After all, it's your world.

5 WAYS TO SAVE MONEY WHEN EATING REALLY REAL FOOD

+ Buy your meat in bulk—share or split among friends and family. Store everything in a chest freezer.

+ Be inspired at the market by what's on sale—shop and freeze. Try to shop local and by season.

+ Reshuffle your priorities—maybe you don't need all those cable channels? Or the latest of the late.

+ Implement the good ol' bartering system! Remember that? It can work! And it can be fun!

+ Realize that you will be able to spend money on good food, instead of the all the medications, supplements and junky beauty products that you are used to! It really can make a difference.

THE HOW?
MINIMAL INGREDIENT RECIPES

All of the recipes in this book are made with minimal ingredients in mind. Simple definitely doesn't mean boring, especially when you focus on using herbs and spices to flavor your dishes. Change things up and try to incorporate a variety of different meats and vegetables. Complicated isn't always better. That's why I encourage you to get started with these recipes that will actually let the food shine through. Work to find healthful foods that you love even more than the rubbish you used to adore. Did somebody say bacon?

WHAT'S INCLUDED AND WHAT'S NOT

I have divided this cookbook into three main chapters: three-, four- and five-ingredient dishes. When creating my recipes, all items are included in the count, except for things like water, salt and pepper, cooking fats, vinegars, and commonly found dried herbs and spices. These are all things that I highly recommend that you stock up on first and have locked and loaded in your pantry at all times. Make the small investment upfront, and then you'll have these mainstay ingredients at the ready when needed. Do you need to go out and buy everything all at once? Heck no, but slowly start building the foundation, as these items are part of a solid basis.

STOCK UP ON THESE!
5 COOKING FATS FOR YOUR KITCHEN

+ Lard (pork fat)

+ Coconut oil

+ Duck fat/and or schmaltz (chicken fat)

+ Tallow (beef fat)

+ Butter/Ghee (from grass-fed cows)

+ Olive oil for salads and low-heat cooking

As many of you know, the media has done a wonderful job of vilifying saturated fats from animals with the low-fat craze that began in the 1980s. Don't be afraid to experiment and try some of these fats in various dishes, ranging from grilled or roasted meats, to potatoes and other cooked vegetables. They offer such a fantastic flavor that will also stand up to higher heat temperatures. These are good fats. These are the ones your body will thank you for eating—stable, delicious and in most cases very affordable. They can keep in your fridge or pantry and be reused.

5 VINEGARS FOR YOUR KITCHEN

+ Balsamic vinegar (regular or flavor infused i.e.: raspberry)
+ Apple cider vinegar (ACV)
+ White wine vinegar
+ Red wine vinegar
+ Sherry vinegar

DRIED HERBS & SPICES

(ones that are bolded are included in the ingredient count, as they are more exotic)

+ Allspice
+ Caraway seeds
+ Cayenne
+ Chili powder
+ Chipotle
+ Cinnamon
+ Cumin (ground)
+ Cumin seeds
+ Dry mustard
+ **Five spice blend**
+ **Garam masala**
+ Garlic
+ Ground ginger
+ **Herbs de provance**
+ Italian seasoning
+ Nutmeg
+ **Pickling spice blend**
+ **Ras el hanout**
+ Red curry powder
+ Red pepper flakes
+ Rosemary
+ Sage
+ **Saffron**
+ Smoked paprika
+ **Tandoori spice**
+ Turmeric
+ Thyme
+ Yellow curry powder

Our spice collection is something that has definitely blossomed over time. Find what works for you. Oftentimes, if you don't have a particular one on hand, you can substitute with something that you do. The majority of these are available at your local co-op, bulk or health food store. If not, there are many online distributors that sell quality spices at reasonable prices. Play around and have fun doing so.

'FROM THE GROCER'

Across the top of every recipe, you will find the all you need shortlist of what items are necessary to make the recipe, excluding water, salt, pepper, cooking fats and select dried herbs and spices. That is just for your reference for a quick glance, but I encourage you to read through the actual recipe before cooking to make sure you are set up with all the other stuff. Just in case. The 'from the grocer' ingredients are bolded and the rest are not. For some of the recipes, you will notice that I have included garnishes and dairy suggestions if you tolerate them, or so desire. Please note that these are solely optional and are not integral to the dish. They are just an added bonus, if you know what I mean.

QUALITY VS. QUANTITY

Whenever possible, we like to focus on choosing quality products for our kitchen. Let's face it, we don't all have time for homemade everything. So when and if we are using store-bought sauces, pastes and other grocery goods, we are "happy hunters." We get great joy in finding local and reputable companies that take pride in using clean ingredients to create their homemade(ish) products. Go ahead, put on your Inspector Gadget coat and look for canned and jarred foods that are simply delicious without all the added gobbledygook.

SIDE NOTES & NUTRIENT DENSITY FACTS

At the bottom of the recipes, you will find a side note section and some nutrient density facts for many of the recipes. Those are little tidbits here and there for your reading pleasure. They may include special instructions or possible modifications for certain recipes. I want to point out that these recipes are not written in stone. We have tested and love them, but if you think you would rather include something else or swap something in that you have on hand...DO IT! That is the beauty of cooking: you can really make it your own based on your preferences.

NOW WHAT?

Now that you have wiped out your pantry and cleared it of all the old processed garbagio (hopefully you have done that), it's time to get crackin'. To do so in a fruitful way, turn to local companies, businesses, farmers markets and actual farms for food sourcing. (Check out my resources!) I urge you to start paying attention to folks who actually have your best interests in mind. Once you have loaded up on what you need, try to refocus your attention to viewing food as just food. It doesn't have to be a set breakfast, lunch and dinner. I inspire you to look at it as ongoing nourishment that you are providing your body throughout the day. Try to alter your views on leftovers as well, as they can be life savers when you are busy and don't have the time to cook every night.

Think about how you can set yourself up for success. Experiment, try, perhaps flop (that's okay), try again and get better along the way. Remember, I used to be the fast food junkie. For some peeps a gradual approach works best. For others, a cold-turkey-dive-right-in entrance into a new way of eating is their style. After all, you know yourself best! Open up your mind, as the possibilities for cooking amazing food are endless. Get inspired, roll up your sleeves and give it a go! Ignore the fact that you hated zucchini as a child and attempt it in a different way. You have the control. Just because you don't like steamed broccoli doesn't mean that you won't love it roasted! Many times, a slightly different mode of preparation or inclusion on ingredients can make all the difference.

In this section I thought about including a meal plan and accompanying grocery list. But, guess what? I decided against it. Not because I wanted to be a meanie, but because I have full faith in you that you can grab a piece a paper and a good ol' pencil and map things out based on your life, your needs and your family. Me telling you what you eat, how to eat it and when to eat it is counterproductive. I believe that the autonomy should come from within. (Who actually cooks all their meals out of one cookbook anyways?) When you have an active role in the planning, ownership for your progress will be more real! Sometimes a zillion guides, plans or groceries lists can leave you feeling overwhelmed. Part of this whole process is gathering recipes and meal ideas that are going to get your family charged and thrilled about eating wholesome foods. My desire is for you to dive in and explore this further.

Life can get busy ... I hear that, but when you feel overwhelmed just ponder, remember and daydream about the days when your biggest concern was where you were going to hang your poster on your bedroom wall. All in jest, but what I will leave you with is this: more isn't always better, and often times less is more. Simplicity rules. Perfection isn't attainable, but change CAN happen. It starts with you! Don't overthink things.

5 WAYS TO STOP, RELAX AND CELEBRATE THE FOOD YOU ARE EATING

+ Sit down & set the table whenever possible. Or at least sit!

+ When you are eating, focus on the beautiful food in front of you (and not your phone). We have started leaving ours at home if we go out for dinner!

+ Become part of the process of creating the food, and you will more than likely savor it as you eat. Grow a garden, volunteer at a farm, help make a meal—you get the idea!

+ When dining, make it an experience whenever possible—you know, talk to the people and have conversation, set the table and light a candle. Simple, yet effective!

+ CHEW and breathe—this will help you to digest as well. True story!

TRY TURNING IT INTO A PASSION

(or at least something that you don't view as a chore!)

Obviously there are nights when you just don't feel like cooking. That's okay. I get it, it's normal. Remember, this is a project about you. See if you can find ways to make cooking an experience rather than a dreaded task. Get your family involved, get your spouse or partner on board, turn on the tunes, chef it up and get pumped about serving up some really real food to your family. Focus on the offerings that you can consume, rather than what you cannot. Most of all, remember just to take it day by day and relax. It's all good. Make the investment. Your life is worth it and so are YOU! Who knows? You may even start to like (read ... love) cooking after all. (That's what happened to me!)

3
INGREDIENTS

The most minimal of the bunch, these 3 ingredient recipes are marked with beauty because of their simplicity. With a less-is-more mentality, these recipes will allow the true flavors of the foods you are using to shine through. Paired to complement one another, each dish will leave you feeling accomplished knowing how little it took to create something purely delicious. Try one of my favorites: the bacon-wrapped rosemary sweet potato fries. It's a one-pan wonder that cooks up into caramelized bundles. Bundles of joy that is—it's literally like the bacon is hugging the sweet potato because it's so happy! If you are celebrating a special occasion, spree for the pork belly. Every time we make this dish, we are greeted with meat that is so juicy, it literally melts in our mouths with the added bonus of a little crispy crunch. Match it with the garlic mashed potatoes and you'll take it over the edge. Up for adventure? Try boiling your own lobster and serving it with parsnip fries dipped in smoked paprika mayonnaise. Is your mouth watering yet? Good! This is just the beginning: read on to find out about more of my makings.

+ BACON-WRAPPED ROSEMARY SWEET POTATO FRIES

+ ZESTY LIME SRIRACHA WINGS

+ CREAMY ROASTED BUTTERNUT SQUASH SOUP WITH GINGER & CILANTRO

+ GINGERED BALSAMIC AND DATE GLAZED CHICKEN LEGS

+ SHAKE 'N' BAKE CHOPS

+ PARSNIP AND CARROT MASH WITH A HINT OF NUTMEG

+ CIDER COLLARD GREENS WITH PANCETTA

+ CLAM CURRIED MUSSELS

+ CHORIZO & KALE WITH SAUTÉED ONIONS

+ PAN-FRIED BASIL PESTO COD

+ PORK BELLY WITH GARLIC MASHED POTATOES

+ SESAME CRUSTED SEA BASS WITH GARLIC-INFUSED BABY SHRIMP

+ ROASTED GARLIC JERUSALEM ARTICHOKES WITH HAZELNUTS

+ LOBSTER WITH TARRAGON PARSNIP FRIES

+ TOMATO BRAISED CHICKEN DISH

+ BLACK PEPPER SEARED AHI TUNA STEAK WITH PICKLED GINGER

+ ROOT VEGETABLE CHIPS WITH COARSE SEA SALT

BACON-WRAPPED ROSEMARY SWEET POTATO FRIES

I distinctly remember the day my husband and I came up with this recipe. We were walking home along the beach and talking about what we'd make for dinner. We knew that we were going to make homemade chicken wings and wanted something super delicious to go along with them. Honestly, who doesn't love the amazing combo of sweet potatoes and bacon? I know we do! The rosemary and hot pepper sauce make these bite-sized morsels totally irresistible. For extra enjoyment, we dipped them in some gorgeous guacamole. Eater beware: highly addictive! They're like candy!

MAKES 4 SERVINGS

4 large **sweet potatoes**, peeled and sliced

1 tbsp (2 g) dried rosemary

1 lb (454 g) good quality **bacon**

a dash of coarse sea salt or flakes

a generous splash of **hot pepper sauce**

Preheat your oven to 350°F (176°C).

Start by peeling and slicing the sweet potatoes into sticks (chunky fry style) and place them in a bowl. Sprinkle with dried rosemary and mix thoroughly using your hands or tongs.

Then take each sweet potato stick and wrap them with slices of bacon on a diagonal. Once wrapped, arrange the sticks evenly on a baking sheet lined with aluminum foil with the loose bacon ends face down.

Bake for 40 minutes, until bacon becomes crispy. If you wish to make them extra crispy, turn the oven to broil for the remaining 5 to 10 minutes. Plate and sprinkle with coarse sea salt. Finish by topping with a splash or two of hot sauce.

+ **SIDE NOTE:** If the bacon is too wide, you can slice it lengthwise so it is easier to wrap around the sweet potato fries!

+ **NUTRIENT DENSITY FACT:** Sweet potatoes are an excellent source of vitamin A, with over 1x the RDA.

ZESTY LIME SRIRACHA WINGS

Folks always seem shocked and somewhat surprised when they find out that they can still enjoy chicken wings while following a paleo lifestyle. The homemade variety is what I am talking about here! So super uncomplicated, they are really no sweat to make at all. As you probably already know, baked chicken wings can be done in a variety of different ways. This wing recipe will bestow a desired crispiness, woven in with a spicy sauce!

MAKES 2 TO 4 SERVINGS

2½ lbs (1.2 kg) **fresh chicken wings**, about 24

2 tbsp (30 mL) olive oil

¼ cup (60 mL) of **hot sauce** (we recommend Sriracha)

1 **lime**, zest and juice

freshly chopped cilantro for garnish

Preheat oven to 375°F (190°C).

Pour all the wings into a large bowl and drizzle with the olive oil. Using tongs, mix thoroughly making sure all of them are coated in the oil. Arrange the wings on your baking sheet lined with aluminum foil.

Bake in oven for approximately 40 to 50 minutes, turning them with tongs every 15 minutes. Once crispy to your liking, pour them back into a clean large glass mixing bowl. Add in the hot sauce and toss again using the tongs to coat evenly.

Discard used aluminum foil and re-line the baking sheet with a new layer of foil. Arrange the wings back on the baking sheet and evenly sprinkle with lime zest. Place baking sheet back into the oven and broil for 5 minutes. Remove from oven and let rest for 5 minutes before serving, as they will be very hot! Drizzle with a little bit of freshly squeezed lime juice and plate. Garnish with freshly chopped cilantro.

+ **SIDE NOTE:** If you want a bit more sauce, feel free to pour some in a small bowl for dipping. Look for a sauce that is an artisanal brand with clean and minimal ingredients. We found ours at the farmers market!

+ **NUTRIENT DENSITY FACT:** Chicken wings are an excellent source of selenium. They are also a good source of iron, phosphorus and vitamin B$_3$.

CREAMY ROASTED BUTTERNUT SQUASH SOUP WITH GINGER & CILANTRO

Smooth, silky and satisfying. This soup will be sure to warm you on one of those days where you just need a little extra comfort. This rich and velvety dish holds an irresistible texture that is very pleasing to the palate. The gorgeous hint of ginger and added bonus of fresh cilantro will tantalize your taste buds with every spoonful. It's a simple dish that holds many benefits such as providing lovely leftovers for the next day and being an affordable way to feed the tummies of your entire family. Pairs well with a side salad for lunch or fill up a mug and enjoy this warmth by itself whenever you are hungry.

MAKES 6+ SERVINGS

2 medium **butternut squash**, halved and gutted

2 tbsp (28 g) coconut oil

1 (1.7 cups [400 mL]) can full fat **coconut milk**

4 cups (950 mL) water

1 to 2 tbsp (7 to 14 g) ground ginger, depending on taste

a handful **fresh cilantro**, chopped

2 tsp (10 g) sea salt

2 tsp (5 g) ground pepper

Preheat oven to 350°F (195°C).

Using a sharp knife, halve and remove the seeds from the butternut squash. You can roast the seeds if you so desire. Brush the flesh side with coconut oil and place face down on a baking sheet lined with aluminum foil. Roast in oven for approximately 45 minutes to 1 hour, until fork tender.

When done, remove and spoon out squash into a Dutch oven pot. Add in can of coconut milk (shake well) and water. Using an immersion hand blender, puree for 5 to 10 minutes until smooth and creamy. Finally, add in ground ginger, fresh cilantro, salt and pepper. Stir thoroughly, making sure all lumps have been dissolved.

If you tolerate dairy, add in some Parmesan or goat cheese and/or use full fat cream.

+ **SIDE NOTE:** If you do not wish to roast the squash, you can peel, cube and boil until softened.

+ **NUTRIENT DENSITY FACT:** Ground ginger packs some serious punch. It is an excellent source of manganese, with over 14x the RDA. It is an excellent source of selenium and iron. Ginger also contains good amounts of copper, magnesium, potassium, zinc, vitamin B_3 and vitamin B_6.

GINGERED BALSAMIC AND DATE GLAZED CHICKEN LEGS

When my husband and I made this recipe for the first time, there may have been a game of rock, paper, scissors in our kitchen to determine who would get the last one! Best two out of three always wins! This simple and easy glaze will leave your family or dinner guests wondering what sweetness just hit their lips. Don't fancy chicken legs? No worries, this glaze works well with chicken thighs, breasts or wings as well.

MAKES 3 SERVINGS

6 **chicken legs/drumsticks**, skin-on

3 tbsp (33 g) cooking fat (we used butter)

8 **fresh dates**, pitted and finely chopped

¾ cup (180 mL) balsamic vinegar

1 tbsp (15 g) **fresh ginger**, grated

½ tsp salt

ground pepper to taste

Preheat oven to 375°F (190°C).

Start by brushing chicken legs with some melted cooking fat. Place the chicken on a rack in a roasting pan and bake for 35 minutes, or until skin becomes crispy (internal temperature of 175°F [79°C]).

In the meantime, puree dates, balsamic vinegar, ginger, salt and pepper in a small food processor. Pulse these ingredients together until a paste has formed. You may have to stop it occasionally and scrape the mixture off the sides, as sometimes the dates can stick.

Transfer the mixture to a small saucepan and heat over medium heat on the stovetop, stirring occasionally until it becomes the consistency of a honey-like glaze. If it is too thick you may have to add in a little bit more balsamic.

Remove the chicken when cooked and brush generously with the date glaze, making sure the entire drumstick is coated. Return to oven and broil for approximately 5 minutes, watching closely. You can use tongs to turn, and broil opposite side if you wish. Let them sit and cool for 5 to 10 minutes before serving.

+ **SIDE NOTE:** The glaze is sweet, so a little goes a long way!

+ **NUTRIENT DENSITY FACT:** Dates are a good source of copper.

SHAKE 'N' BAKE CHOPS

If you are a '70s baby you will probably remember eating Shake 'n' Bake chops back in the day. You know, the kind where you would buy the premade spices in a box, open up a pack, throw it all in a plastic bag, give it a shaky-shake and bake away. I recall it like it was yesterday! I used to love that. My siblings and I used to argue over who would get to lick the crumbs out of the bag. Gross, eh? Try these super straightforward chops that crisp up nicely in the oven and will perhaps bring you back to your childhood.

MAKES 4 SERVINGS

4 **pork chops,** (1.5 lbs [680 g]) bone in

2 tsp (10 g) sea salt

2 **eggs**, whisked

1 cup (90 g) **almond flour**

¼ cup (60 g) Italian seasoning (dried oregano, marjoram, thyme, rosemary, basil and sage)

Place chops on a wire racked baking sheet. Salt and allow time to sit and then pat dry to remove some of the moisture. Start by whisking eggs together in a medium glass bowl to create an egg wash. In a separate bowl, combine the almond flour and dried herbs.

Next, take pork chops and dip/dredge in egg. After that, submerge the pork chop in the bowl with all the dry ingredients and completely coat on all sides or shake in a plastic bag. Place in the fridge for 30 minutes to 1 hour. This helps the coating to set and stick well during the cooking process.

Preheat oven to 350°F (176°C).

Place on wire racked baking sheet, and bake in the oven for 30 minutes at 350°F (176°C). Turn the oven up to 375°F (190°), and bake for another 10 minutes or so. For extra crispiness broil for an additional 3 to 5 minutes, watching carefully! Remove from oven, and let cool for 5 minutes before serving.

+ **NUTRIENT DENSITY FACT:** Ground almonds are an excellent source of copper, manganese and vitamin E, all of which are approximately 1x the RDA. They are a very good source of magnesium, phosphorus and vitamin B_2 as well as a good source of iron and vitamin B_3.

PARSNIP AND CARROT MASH WITH A HINT OF NUTMEG

Creamy, smooth and buttery in texture, this side will work well with many main dishes and is a welcomed alternative to your regular mashed potatoes. Adding a pinch of nutmeg releases a complementary flavor that is a solid affinity to its counterparts. Using an immersion hand blender is a must in this dish, as it ensures a consistency that is worth writing home about.

MAKES 4+ SERVINGS

3 **parsnips**, peeled and cut into chunks

6 **carrots**, peeled and cut into small chunks

6 cups (1.4 L) water

⅓ cup (80 mL) **chicken broth**

3 tbsp (43 g) butter

¼ tsp nutmeg

½ tsp sea salt

¼ tsp ground pepper

freshly chopped parsley or chives for garnish

Place parsnips and the carrots in a large Dutch oven and cover them with water. Bring to a boil over high heat. With the lid on, cook for 15 to 20 minutes on high heat, or until the vegetables have softened. Check doneness with a fork.

Turn down the stovetop to medium low heat. Pour out most of the water, leaving only a little bit. Add in broth, butter, nutmeg, salt and pepper.

Using an immersion hand blender, mix all the ingredients until a puree is formed (don't be shy about giving your arms a workout here because a very creamy consistency is your goal). Garnish with freshly chopped parsley or chives.

+ **SIDE NOTE:** If the mash seems too thick, you can continue whipping while adding in a bit more broth or butter to make it even creamier! Carrots typically take a little bit longer to cook than parsnips, so cut them in smaller chunks.

+ **NUTRIENT DENSITY FACT:** Nutmeg is an excellent source of copper and manganese, with both just over 1x the RDA. It is also a good source of iron, magnesium, phosphorus and vitamin B_1.

CIDER COLLARD GREENS WITH PANCETTA

The first time I tried collard greens was during a trip in New Orleans. The second time was at a BBQ joint in Boston while we were on vacation and visiting Mat Lalonde. Both experiences were impressive, leaving me with the notion of, "Hey, I could easily make these myself!" It's a peppy side dish that just makes me happy while chowing down on some ribs, wings or pulled pork. Look for these rich, dark leafy greens in the produce section of your health food store. The pancetta, red pepper flakes and cider vinegar are quite the trio. They come together to create a party in the mouth with this one!

MAKES 4 SERVINGS

4 to 6 thick slices **pancetta**, cut into small chunks

1 small **yellow onion**, finely diced

2 bunches **collard greens**, stems removed and cut into ribbons

1 tsp red pepper flakes

sea salt and ground pepper to taste

2 tbsp (30 mL) apple cider vinegar

In a large cast-iron skillet, cook the pancetta over medium to high heat on the stovetop. Allow the pancetta to cook for 15 minutes or until the chunks become slightly crispy. Use tongs to turn them over during this process. Scoop them out when done, using a slotted spoon and set aside in a small glass bowl.

Keep the remaining pork fat from the pancetta in the skillet. Turn the heat down to medium-low and begin to cook and stir the onion, until softened. Add in the collard greens, red pepper flakes and salt and pepper, stirring well in order to mix everything together and coat with the pork fat.

Stir back in the bits of pancetta and add the cider vinegar. Cook covered over medium heat for about 30 minutes or until the collard greens are completely softened.

If you tolerate dairy, add in some Parmesan cheese.

+ **SIDE NOTE:** The key ingredient in this dish is the apple cider vinegar—it's very complementary, thus I wouldn't recommend subbing it with another kind of vinegar. When raw, it'll seem like A LOT of greens but they reduce a ton when cooking!

+ **NUTRIENT DENSITY FACT:** Collard greens are an excellent source of vitamin K, with approximately 5x the RDA. They are also a very good source of vitamin A and a good source of vitamin C.

CLAM CURRIED MUSSELS

Love seafood? Love soup? Then this pairing is the best of both worlds. Enjoy scooping up
this Indian-inspired broth with these bite-sized tidbits from the sea. The tomato expands this dish
to give it even more structure with every bite. Not familiar with red curry powder? Don't worry, it
can easily be found at grocery stores in the international cuisine section. Its use is unforgettable,
as it provides a lovely color and a distinct taste that works hand-in-hand with this dish.
An easy weeknight dinner that takes no time at all!

MAKES 2 TO 3 SERVINGS

2 cups (475 mL) **clam juice**

1 (1¾ cups [398 mL]) can **diced tomatoes**

2 tsp (7 g) red curry powder

½ tsp sea salt

¼ tsp ground pepper

2 lbs (908 g) **mussels**, cleaned and de-bearded

freshly chopped parsley for garnish

Rinse, scrub and de-beard the mussels. In a large Dutch oven, pour in clam juice, diced tomatoes and red curry powder. Bring to a boil, stirring occasionally. Reduce heat to medium and add salt and pepper. Pour in mussels and cook covered for 10 to 12 minutes.

Remove lid and check to make sure mussels are done and have opened up nicely. Divide mussels into portions and cover with liquid broth. Feel free to garnish with some freshly chopped parsley.

+ **SIDE NOTE:** The clam juice really adds a nice touch; it can be found in a large can at your local seafood market. Feel free to adjust the amount of red curry spice accordingly, depending on your preference. Start with recommended amount and taste test as you go, adding more if needed! Discard any mussels that don't open.

+ **NUTRIENT DENSITY FACT:** Mussels are an excellent source of iron, selenium and manganese. They are especially rich in vitamin B_{12}, with over 10x the RDA. They are also a good source of phosphorus, zinc and vitamin B_1 and vitamin B_2.

CHORIZO AND KALE WITH SAUTÉED ONIONS

The simplicity of this dish is what really comes through with this recipe. Don't you just adore those instances when you can throw everything together on the stovetop and presto...an amazing dish has been mastered? If chorizo isn't your thing, feel free to sub in whatever type of sausage suits your fancy. This dish is solid as a morning feast, midday snack or as some evening eats.

MAKES 4 SERVINGS

4 **chorizo sausage**, coined

1 tbsp (14 g) coconut oil

1 large **yellow onion**, sliced

1 bunch green curly **kale**, chopped into ribbons

sea salt and ground pepper to taste

In a large heavy cast-iron skillet, cook sausage over medium to high heat, turning coins when browned. After cooking them for about 10 minutes per side, set aside. At the same time, in another skillet, heat cooking oil over medium heat. Sauté the onions until they become translucent or softened. Combine both the sausage and the onions back into the cast-iron skillet and add in your kale by the handful, stirring occasionally. Season with salt and pepper and cook altogether for another 10 minutes.

+ **NUTRIENT DENSITY FACT:** Kale is an excellent source of vitamin A and K. It has approximately 7x the RDA for vitamin K. It is also a good source of vitamin C.

PAN-FRIED BASIL PESTO COD

This white fish sports delicious basil pesto and red potatoes. For this recipe, they must be reds and keep the skins on. This is a sure-fire dish that will charm your dinner guests. The cod is mild and flaky and takes in all the twang of the pesto. Feel free to make your own or look for a minimal ingredient option in a store near you!

MAKES 2 SERVINGS

3 **red potatoes**, with skin on, quartered

6 cups (1.4 L) water

4 tbsp (57 g) cooking fat, divided (we used butter)

2 (½ lb [227 g]) **cod fillets**, skin removed

½ tsp sea salt

½ tsp ground pepper

½ cup (118 mL) **basil pesto**, store bought, divided

a squeeze of fresh lemon for garnish

Place the potatoes in a large Dutch oven and cover with water. Bring the water to boil. Reduce heat to medium-high, cover and cook until potatoes are fork tender. Drain the water and keep the potatoes in the Dutch oven with the lid on until ready to serve. This will help keep them warm.

Melt 2 tablespoons (28.5 g) of butter in a large non-stick skillet over medium heat. Prepare fish by seasoning with salt and pepper on both sides. Place the fillets presentation side down in the skillet first and pan-fry for 2 to 3 minutes depending on thickness. With a thin lifter, carefully turn the fish over and continue to fry the other side for another 2 to 3 minutes

At the same time that you are cooking the cod, heat another 2 tablespoons (28.5 g) of butter in a small saucepan over low to medium heat. Add in half the basil pesto and heat for 3 minutes, stirring together.

Finish the dish by scooping out desired amount of potatoes, and toss them in half of the basil pesto to coat. The potatoes will be plated on the side. Next, plate the cod fillet and then drizzle with the remaining pesto sauce. Finish with a squeeze of lemon juice.

If you tolerate dairy, add some Gruyere cheese.

+ NUTRIENT DENSITY FACT: Cod is a very good source of selenium; it is also a good source of vitamin B_{12}.

PORK BELLY WITH GARLIC MASHED POTATOES

We had our first pork belly experience when we were out for dinner with friends. This is a salty, melt-in-your-mouth, unbelievable-with-each-bite kind of venture. The pork belly we had was a braised dish. Although we absolutely loved it, we thought it would be interesting to try a crispy skinned version. This substantial dish is best served as an appetizer cut into long strips or as a main over a milky mashed vegetable. It holds incredible flavor within the layer of succulent fat and meat with a crispy top layer of skin. Look for a weighty piece of pork belly at your local butcher shop. Kindly ask them to keep the skin on, as this is what will give you that outer sheet of crackling brittle.

MAKES 4 SERVINGS

FOR THE BRINE

12 cups (2.8 L) water

4 tbsp (60 mL) vinegar of choice (we used ACV)

3 cloves **fresh garlic**

½ tbsp cumin seeds

4 dried bay leaves

1 tbsp (8 g) black peppercorns

½ tsp paprika

½ tbsp (8 g) sea salt

FOR THE PORK BELLY

2 lbs (908 g) **pork belly**, with skin on

1 tbsp (15 mL) apple cider vinegar

1 tsp sea salt

FOR THE GARLIC MASHED POTATOES

6 cups (1.4 L) water

18 **mini white new potatoes,** halved

4 cloves **fresh garlic**, minced

3 tbsp (43 g) butter

½ tsp sea salt

½ tsp ground pepper

(continued)

Combine the brine ingredients in a large Dutch oven. Bring to a boil. Once it reaches a rumbling boil, remove it from the heat and let cool. Then place the pork belly in the brine and let sit in the refrigerator overnight.

The next day, remove pork belly from brine. Place on a cutting board and pat dry. Using the tip of a sharp knife carefully score the skin of the pork belly (you do not want to create deep cuts in the meat though, so do this fairly gently). Drizzle with apple cider vinegar and rub with a generous amount of sea salt. Use your hands to really make sure this mixture is being rubbed in well.

Preheat your oven to 425°F (218°C).

Place pork belly on a wire-racked roasting pan and cook for the first 35 minutes at that temperature. Then reduce the oven temperature to 375°F (190°C) for 15 minutes; then to 325°F (162°C) for another 15 minutes; then to 275°F (135°C) for the last 15 minutes. Total cooking time will be 1 hour and 20 minutes. If you feel that it still needs to get a little bit crispier, cook for another 5 to 10 minutes back up at 375°F (190°C). When the skin is nice and crispy on top you know that your pork belly is done. Check by tapping it with a metal fork for hardness. Let cool for 5 minutes.

In the meantime, prepare your mashed potatoes so that they are done at the same time as the pork belly. Start by placing potatoes in a large Dutch oven and cover with water. On the stovetop, bring to a boil over high heat. Cook potatoes until fork tender. Remove from heat and drain water. Place back on the stove and turn the heat down to low. With an immersion hand blender or a hand masher, puree the potatoes until they reach your desired consistency. Add in butter, garlic, salt and pepper. Using a large spoon, whip everything together.

Using a serrated knife, cut the pork belly into slices, strips or cubes. Serve on top of mashed potatoes.

+ **SIDE NOTE:** Cook the pork belly slowly and gently in order to get that crackling, delicious skin. Purchase more than you think you will need from the butcher, as the pork belly will shrink some while it is roasting—probably about ⅓ or ½ of its original size. Wanna switch it up? Try substituting the purple potatoes or purple yams for the white potatoes. They become a pretty light lavender color when mashed.

+ **NUTRIENT DENSITY FACT:** Pork belly is a very good source of selenium. It is also a good source of copper and zinc.

SESAME CRUSTED SEA BASS WITH GARLIC-INFUSED BABY SHRIMP

So flavorful and silky, your palate won't believe that this fish dish is such a minimal ingredient meal. The sesame seeds add a lovely crunch and slight nuttiness that adheres so nicely to the outer flesh of the bass. Topping this fillet with a generous spoonful of the garlic sautéed baby shrimp is a pairing that will delight your senses. Simple does it—a side of steamed vegetables would work well here, too!

MAKES 2 SERVINGS

¼ cup (40 g) **sesame seeds**

2 (½ lb [227 g]) **sea bass fillets**

1 tsp sea salt

½ tsp ground pepper

2 tbsp (30 mL) olive oil

1 tbsp (14 g) cooking fat (we used butter or ghee)

½ package of **baby shrimp** (½ cup [340 g])

1 tsp garlic powder

a squeeze of fresh lemon juice for garnish

Pour the sesame seeds on a cutting board, forming a single layer. Start by seasoning the fish with salt and pepper. Take each fillet and lay it into the layer of sesame seeds, turning to make sure that all the sides are covered in the seeds.

In a large cast-iron skillet, heat olive oil over medium heat. Gently place the fillets in the skillet and cook on each side for 5 to 7 minutes total. You want to do this slow and steady so as to not burn the sesame seeds. When golden brown, turn fillet over using a thin lifter and repeat on the second side.

At the same time melt cooking fat over medium heat in a separate skillet. Once the fish has been turned and you are on to cooking the second side, begin sautéing the shrimp. Toss in the shrimp. Stir while adding in the garlic powder. Sauté the shrimp over low to medium heat for about 5 minutes.

When both skillets are ready, plate the fish fillet first and top with a spoonful of shrimp. Garnish with a squeeze of fresh lemon.

+ NUTRIENT DENSITY FACTS:

+ Sesame seeds are nutrient dense little guys. They are an excellent source of calcium, iron, magnesium, manganese, phosphorus and most of all: copper. They have approximately 4x the RDA for copper. They are also a very good source of selenium, zinc and vitamins B_1, B_6 and B_3.

+ Sea bass is an excellent source of vitamin B12 and selenium, as well as a good source of phosphorus.

ROASTED GARLIC JERUSALEM ARTICHOKES WITH HAZELNUTS

I remember trying Jerusalem artichokes (also known as sunchokes) for the first time when we received them in a mixed vegetable box from our local CSA. To be honest, at the time, I really didn't know too much about them. That was about to change, as there were a few little guys hanging out among some root vegetables and tubers. You can find these yummy things at most markets—they sort of look like fresh ginger! Once roasted, these wee tubers turn out to be deliciously nutty and have basically the same inside texture as that of a white potato. When paired with roasted garlic and chopped hazelnuts, you end up with a hearty dish. I highly recommend finishing it off with a sprinkling of good quality goat cheese.

MAKES 4 SERVINGS

¼ cup (39 g) raw **hazelnuts,** roasted, skins removed and chopped

2 heads **fresh garlic**, outer skin removed

3 tbsp (45 mL) olive oil, divided

¾ tsp sea salt, divided

¾ tsp ground pepper, divided

2 lbs (908 g) **Jerusalem artichokes**, chopped into 1" (2½ cm) pieces

Preheat oven to 350°F (176°C).

Spread out hazelnuts on a baking sheet and roast for 3 to 5 minutes, watching carefully to make sure that the majority of the skins are starting to split. Remove from oven, and place into a tea towel. Rub vigorously to remove the skins. Place in a small glass bowl and set aside for later.

Turn oven temperature up to 375°F (190°C). Remove outer layer of skin from the garlic and chop off ¼ inch (.6 cm) off the top and discard. Place each head of garlic on a piece of aluminum foil. Drizzle with 1 tablespoon (15 mL) of olive oil and ¼ teaspoon salt and pepper. Bring sides together and twist together at the top to close. Place each package in the oven on the rack and roast for 20 minutes.

In the meantime, take the jerusalem artichokes and put them into a large glass bowl. Pour in 2 tablespoons (30 mL) of olive oil and ½ teaspoon of salt and pepper. Using tongs, toss together to ensure they are coated.

Pour them into a deep baking pan and transfer the garlic packages into the pan alongside the artichokes. Bake for 25 minutes all together, stirring regularly until browned. Bake until cooked through, but not mushy! Plate by scooping out potions of artichokes first, adding in a few cloves of roasted garlic and topping with a sprinkling of chopped hazelnuts.

If you tolerate dairy, add in some goat cheese.

+ **NUTRIENT DENSITY FACT:** Hazelnuts are an excellent source of copper and vitamin E, with both at approximately 1x the RDA. They are also a very good source of manganese and a good source of iron, phosphorus, vitamin B_1 and B_6.

LOBSTER WITH TARRAGON PARSNIP FRIES

Lobster. It's always impressive at restaurants, but feared by many home cooks. Be afraid no longer, and don't be intimidated, as boiling lobster in a large stockpot is super simple in reality. They take no time at all and can be enjoyed in so many ways. Oh, and contrary to popular myth, they do not squeal or try to escape during this whole process. My sister-in-law, Christina, recommended pairing them with parsnip fries. What a super suggestion! We took it one step further and enjoyed this dish with the added bonus of homemade smoked sweet paprika mayonnaise.

MAKES 2 SERVINGS

enough water to fill a large stock pot ½ to ¾ of the way full

2 tbsp (30 g) sea salt for every quart of water you use

2 (1¼ lbs [567 g]) **lobsters**

4 **parsnips**, peeled and cut into sticks

3 tbsp (43 g) cooking fat, melted (we used ghee)

2 tbsp (4 g) chopped **fresh tarragon**

sea salt and ground pepper, to taste

FOR THE LOBSTER

Fill your stockpot ½ to ¾ of the way full of water. Cover and bring to a boil over high heat. Take your live lobster, cut off the elastic bands from the claws and submerge it headfirst into the water once you have reached a boil. Do this while carefully holding the middle of the body before releasing the lobster completely.

Start monitoring your cooking time once the water has come back to a boil. Cook each lobster for 8 to 10 minutes, uncovered. Remove using tongs and carefully place on a platter to cool.

FOR THE TARRAGON PARSNIP FRIES

Preheat oven to 350°F (176°C).

Place cut parsnips into a large glass bowl. Add in cooking fat, toss in the fresh tarragon and sprinkle to taste with salt and pepper. Mix it all together thoroughly using tongs, making sure that everything is coated well. Line a baking sheet with parchment paper or aluminum foil. Spread your parsnip strips out on the sheet in one layer. Bake in the oven for 25 to 35 minutes, turning halfway through the process. After they cook, remove them with tongs and place on a wire rack to cool. Some, which are smaller, may cook faster than others. Enjoy by dipping in some smoked paprika mayo—see page 206.

+ **SIDE NOTE:** Depending on the size of your pot, you can boil the lobsters separately or together. We like to cook ours separately to ensure greater accuracy with cooking times.

+ **NUTRIENT DENSITY FACT:** Lobster is an excellent source of copper and selenium, approximately the full RDA of these two minerals per every ¾ cup (100 g) portion. It's also a very good source of vitamins A and B$_{12}$ and a good source of phosphorus, zinc and vitamin B5.

TOMATO BRAISED CHICKEN DISH

One day I arrived home with the ever persistent angst of what I would make for dinner. I proceeded to open the fridge and to my astonished eyes I found a very large container of grape tomatoes, two and a half pounds to be exact! Also in the maze of the refrigerator I discovered several chicken breasts. With fear of the refrigerator vortex swallowing me whole, I quickly shut the door. My thoughts were obviously of what to do with chicken and tomatoes, and I quickly set to work. Braising the chicken and creating lovely browned bits on the pan led me to adding the sweet and luscious tomatoes to lift all the scrumptious pieces. Before long we were at the table enjoying tomato braised chicken.

MAKES 4+ SERVINGS

3 tbsp (42 g) cooking fat, divided (we used coconut oil)

6 **chicken breasts** bone in, skinless

sea salt and ground pepper, to taste

1 tbsp (7 g) garlic powder

1 yellow **onion**, chopped

3 (1 lb [454 g]) containers of **grape tomatoes**, cut in half

½ cup (120 mL) of balsamic vinegar

1 tbsp (3 g) of Italian seasoning

Preheat oven to 350°F (176°C).

In a large cast-iron skillet, melt 2 tablespoons (28 g) cooking fat over high heat. Season chicken with salt, pepper and garlic powder. Gently place each piece into the skillet and sear, turning and browning on all sides while keeping the temperature of the pan hot—about 10 minutes total.

Remove chicken from skillet when nicely browned and set aside. In the meantime, melt 1 tablespoon (14 g) cooking fat in a large Dutch oven over medium to high heat. Add in onion and stir and cook for 5 to 10 minutes, until softened. Then add in tomatoes and continue to cook for another 5 to 10 minutes. Pour in balsamic vinegar and Italian seasoning and mix together thoroughly. Simmer for 5 minutes on low heat.

Add the chicken to the Dutch oven and spoon the mixture overtop, making sure it is coated well. Place it in the oven, cover and bake for 35 minutes. Divide into portions and plate.

+ **NUTRIENT DENSITY FACT:** Chicken breasts are a good source of copper, phosphorus, selenium and vitamin B_3.

BLACK PEPPER SEARED AHI TUNA STEAK WITH PICKLED GINGER

For the longest time, I was just an eater of good ol' canned tuna! Since then, searing tuna steaks honestly made me love this fish even more. All it takes is creating a ground pepper crust, a little sear on both sides and Bob's your uncle. That's it...that's all folks! The searing process is not meant as a cook-all-the-way-through kind of deal. You want to have that crispy outside with an inside that's pretty much rare. That's where the importance of sourcing a sashimi grade tuna comes in. This buttery fish will be sure to pretty much melt with every single bite you take.

MAKES 2 SERVINGS

2 (½ lb [227 g]) **ahi tuna steaks** (1" [2½ cm] thick)

½ cup (120 mL) **coconut aminos**

1 to 2 tsp of ground pepper

1 tbsp (15 mL) cooking fat (we used olive oil)

4 tbsp (20 g) fresh **pickled ginger**

a squeeze of fresh lemon juice and wasabi for garnish

Place tuna steaks in a large re-sealable bag or casserole dish and pour in the coconut aminos. Let marinate for at least 30 minutes before cooking. When ready to cook, remove from the refrigerator and place the tuna steaks on a cutting board, letting them come to room temperature. Next, season with a generous amount of pepper on both sides of the fish.

In a non-stick skillet, heat cooking fat over medium to high heat. Wait for the pan to get hot and then carefully place the tuna steaks in the pan. Sear the fish on the first side for 2 to 3 minutes, or until you have achieved a nice crust. Using tongs, gently turn the tuna steak over. Continue to sear the tuna on the other side for the same amount of time.

Once seared (remember, you do not want to cook it all the way through) let sit for 5 minutes on a cutting board. Using a sharp knife, slice thinly and serve. Top with fresh pickled ginger. Garnish with a squeeze of fresh lemon juice and wasabi.

+ NUTRIENT DENSITY FACTS:

+ Ahi tuna is an excellent source of selenium, vitamin B_3 and B_{12}. It is also a very good source of vitamin B_6 and a good source of phosphorus. It is important to note that tuna contains some vitamin D, which is not commonly found in food.

+ Although typically consumed in smaller quantities, ground black pepper is an excellent source of copper, iron, and vitamin K—over 1x the RDA in all three. Pepper is especially rich in manganese with over 5x the RDA and is also a good source of calcium, magnesium and vitamin B_5.

ROOT VEGETABLE CHIPS WITH COARSE SEA SALT

These chips are made from some of the finest vegetables found below the earth and honestly just make me chipper—pun intended! How many mouths you need to feed will obviously affect the number of vegetables you want to put through the mandolin slicer. It's really up to you … go with it and eyeball it as you go! During the frying process, practice patience and turn them regularly. I don't know why, but this process actually becomes methodically fun. Flip regularly until they start to curl. Coarse sea salt is the commander of this dish, so delicately sprinkle it on the vegetables as soon as they are out of the oil. Ravage this crunch with your favorite dip or unaccompanied. Both are so good!

MAKES 4+ SERVINGS

1 cup (224 g) cooking fat (we used coconut oil)

4 **purple yams**, peeled and thinly sliced

4 **yuca root/cassava**, peeled and thinly sliced

4 **heirloom beets**, thinly sliced

dash of coarse sea salt

In a large cast-iron skillet, heat your cooking fat over medium to high heat. You will always want to make sure that there is about ¼ inch (.6 cm) covering the bottom of the pan at all times.

Slice vegetables with the mandolin slicer on the middle setting. Put all sliced vegetables in a large glass bowl so they are ready to go. To begin a batch, gently place your slices in the oil. Using tongs, flip them over once the edges start to curl and get crispy.

When they are done, remove from the cooking oil using tongs and place them on a wire rack. Salt them and sprinkle with desired herbs and spices (optional) and allow them to cool and get even crunchier before eating! It'll be hard though, because they are so darn yummy!

4 INGREDIENTS

As you browse through this chapter, you will be presented with more than thirty different recipes made up of 4 ingredients. The straightforwardness and uncomplicatedness of these dishes will provide you with many options for quick weeknight meals, as well as possibilities for weekend eats. Want something packed full of loads of vitamins and minerals? Look no further than our freshly shucked oysters that are served with playful mignonettes. To satisfy your BBQ cravings, give the maple chipotle glazed ribs a whirl. I may have eaten an entire rack myself! If you want something a little more off the beaten path, take a crack at the beef tongue or the steak smothered in rosemary bone marrow butter. Both filled with healthful gelatinous properties that will be sure to please.

+ FIVE SPICE BEEF TENDERLOIN WITH THYME BALSAMIC MUSHROOMS

+ TANDOORI CORNISH HENS

+ MAHI MAHI FISH KEBAB WITH GRILLED PINEAPPLE

+ BACON-CRUSTED CHICKEN STRIPS

+ SLOW & STEADY SPICED PORK SHOULDER

+ DUCK FAT CABBAGE WITH PORK & CARAWAY SEEDS

+ MUSTARD-CRUSTED SALMON

+ PAN-FRIED CHICKEN LIVERS WITH PORK LARDONS

+ MARINATED AND BAKED CHICKEN THIGHS—3 WAYS

+ APPLE AND CABBAGE COLESLAW WITH DRIED TART CHERRIES

+ SWEET POTATO AND YAM CRUSTED SPINACH AND CHORIZO QUICHE

+ SAGE-INFUSED MUSTARD AND ONION PORK CHOPS

+ SALMON, EGGS AND ASPARAGUS OVER BUTTERY BIBB LETTUCE

+ PAN-FRIED SOLE WITH MUSHROOM AND TARRAGON SAUCE

+ MUSHROOM AND SAUSAGE BEEF ROLL

+ BUTTERY LAMB CHOPS INFUSED WITH MINT AND LEMON

+ ZUCCHINI, FENNEL AND SARDINES IN MARINARA SAUCE

+ BALSAMIC AND FIG PORK TENDERLOIN

+ MAPLE CHIPOTLE GLAZED BABY BACK PORK RIBS

+ ROASTED DUCK BREAST WITH GINGERED CHERRY SAUCE

+ SAUTÉED ENDIVE WITH SHRIMP AND RUBY RED GRAPEFRUIT

+ OYSTERS WITH MIGNONETTES—3 WAYS

+ CURRIED EGG SALAD

+ SHAVED ROAST BEEF SALAD WITH MARINATED ARTICHOKE HEARTS

+ VENISON WITH JUNIPER BERRY AND POMEGRANATE SAUCE

+ CHICKEN HEART SKEWERS WITH CHIMICHURRI SAUCE

+ LITTLENECK CLAMS WITH SHALLOT AND GARLIC BUTTER

+ DOUBLE-DECKER NACHOS

+ STRIP LOIN STEAK WITH ROASTED GARLIC AND ROSEMARY BONE MARROW BUTTER

+ PEAR AND PROSCIUTTO SALAD WITH TOASTED PINE NUTS

+ ROASTED CAULIFLOWER WITH RAISINS AND PINE NUTS

+ SHREDDED BEEF TONGUE

FIVE SPICE BEEF TENDERLOIN WITH THYME BALSAMIC MUSHROOMS

Enjoy this more lavish cut of meat as part of a special celebration with loved ones or perhaps for a Sunday or holiday dinner. To help protect the pocket book a little bit, look to buying beef tenderloin at your local farmers market or butcher shop when it's a special or on sale. Remember to pull out your handy-dandy meat thermometer for this one, as you want to cook it to perfection.

MAKES 2 TO 4 SERVINGS

1½ lbs (680 g) **beef tenderloin** roast

2 tbsp (29 g) cooking fat (we used butter/ghee)

2 tsp (7 g) **five spice blend**

2 tbsp (6 g) chopped **fresh thyme**, divided

2 (8 oz [226 g]) packages **baby bella mushrooms**, keep whole

½ cup (120 mL) balsamic vinegar

sea salt and ground pepper to taste

Preheat oven to 425°F (218°C).

Remove beef from fridge and carefully trim off any silver skin lining with a sharp knife. Let it sit for about 30 minutes, bringing the meat to room temperature. Pat it dry with a paper towel before applying the rub to the meat.

In a saucepan or microwave, melt cooking fat and pour into a small bowl. Add in the five spice blend and half of the chopped thyme leaves and whisk together. Using a silicone brush, coat all sides of the meat.

Place a large cast-iron skillet over high heat. When the pan is hot, sear all sides of the beef tenderloin—about 1 minute per side. Use tongs to turn and stabilize the meat, making sure all sides have had a chance to form a brown "crust" on the outside.

Transfer the beef to a wire-racked baking pan and roast in the oven for 40 minutes, or until your meat thermometer reads 125°F (51°C). Remove from the oven, and let sit (tented with aluminum foil) on a wooden cutting board for 10 minutes. Slice on an angle against the grain using a sharp knife and serve.

Halfway through your cooking time, prepare the accompanying mushrooms on the stovetop. Do this in the same skillet that you seared the meat. Heat the skillet over medium to high heat, and sauté the mushrooms for 10 minutes. At that point, pour in the balsamic vinegar and other half of chopped thyme, and salt and pepper. Continue to cook and stir for another 10 minutes. Serve as a side or over the top of the sliced beef tenderloin.

+ **NUTRIENT DENSITY FACT:** Beef is an excellent source of iron, phosphorus, selenium, zinc and vitamin B_{12}. It is also a good source of vitamins B_2, B_3, B_5 and B_6.

TANDOORI CORNISH HENS

A multitude of various dried spices pair well with the Cornish hen. I love using our favorite tandoori spice blend in this dish. It is a composite of 17 different spices, all found within one adorable little tin. I highly recommend it as a staple that should be in your pantry because of its versatility. It works amazingly well on poultry, fish and beef. Enjoy the juiciness of this personal-sized bird that is infused with lemon and garlic from the inside out and coated with ghee and spices that create a sweet-scented crust that is finger-licking good!

MAKES 2 SERVINGS

2 (1 lb [454 g]) **Cornish hens**

6 cloves **fresh garlic**, whole

1 **lemon**, sliced into wedges

2 tbsp (28 g) cooking fat, melted (we used ghee)

2 tbsp (16 g) **tandoori spice blend**

Preheat your oven to 375°F (190°C).

Prepare the Cornish hens by stuffing the cavity with cloves of garlic and lemon wedges. Place both hens on a wire-racked baking pan.

In a small glass bowl, combine the ghee and the dried tandoori spices, whisking together. Using a silicone brush, coat the outside of the skin with the mixture—making sure to get in all the crevices.

Cook the hens for 50 minutes or until internal temperature has reached 165°F (73°C). Remove and cover for 5 to 10 minutes, then serve.

MAHI MAHI FISH KEBAB WITH GRILLED PINEAPPLE

When you hear the words mahi mahi, don't they make you think of nice weather? Inspired by this notion, I decided to pair this fish with the beloved tropical fruit: the pineapple. Marinating the fish beforehand is a nice touch—one that gives it that little extra bounce of citrus flavor. From there you have two options. You can either grill the fish and the pineapple in an alternating pattern on each skewer or you can group them in separate corners and grill all the mahi mahi on one side and all the pineapple on the other for more accurate cooking times. Whichever you choose, this combo is nothing short of perfection.

MAKES 2 TO 3 SERVINGS

FOR THE MARINADE

¼ cup (60 mL) olive oil

¼ cup (60 mL) freshly squeezed **orange juice**

2 tbsp (6 g) **Herbs de Provence**

½ tsp ground pepper

1 lb (454 g) **mahi mahi**, cut into 1" (2½ cm) cubes

½ large **pineapple**, cut into similar sized cubes

2 tbsp (30 mL) olive oil, for coating the grill pan

Freshly chopped cilantro and a squeeze of lemon juice and citrus slices for garnish

To prepare the fish for the marinade, cut the fillet(s) into 1 inch by 1 inch (2½ by 2½ cm) cubes. Create the marinade by combining olive oil, orange juice, Herbs de Provence and pepper in a re-sealable bag. Add in the fish and mix together. Let marinate in the refrigerator for a minimum of 30 minutes.

When ready, remove fish from the refrigerator and begin to assemble your skewers. Using either metal or wooden skewers, start by poking a hole through the middle of each piece of fish and pineapple and push them tightly together onto the skewers.

Coat the grill pan with oil and heat over medium heat on the stovetop. These can also be grilled on an outside BBQ if you wish (our prefered method). Gently place the skewers on the grill and let cook on the first side for 2 to 3 minutes. Carefully turn and rotate the pieces on the skewers, making sure all sides have a chance to cook for the same amount of time or maybe a little less (depending on the temperature of your grill).

When done, remove from heat and place them nicely on to a small platter. Garnish with freshly chopped cilantro a squeeze of lemon, and various citrus slices.

+ **SIDE NOTE:** When putting together your skewers, make sure you pack them fairly tightly as this helps them from falling off. If you use metal skewers, they will cook slightly faster than wooden ones. If using wooden ones, make sure to soak skewers in water for 30 minutes beforehand.

+ **NUTRIENT DENSITY FACT:** Mahi mahi is an excellent source of selenium. It is also a good source of vitamins B_3, B_6, and B_{12}.

BACON-CRUSTED CHICKEN STRIPS

As a former fast food eater who loved chicken nuggets, this main makes me smile with such pride and accomplishment. Relish the fact that this homemade version of crunchy, crispy pleasures has been created with healthier ingredients. Feel free to cut them into long strips or into smaller chunks for the kiddos. Served up as a yummy treat, this dish is a phenomenal option if you are hosting a party or making a big platter of goodies while watching sports. For extra bliss, dip these chicken chunks into your favorite BBQ sauce. We found a super clean, store-bought one at our local farmers market with pure ingredients. No added sugar or extra "junk." Have a look around or make your own!

MAKES 2 SERVINGS

1 lb (454 g) **bacon**, crumbled

1 cup (90 g) **almond flour**

1 tsp smoked paprika

½ tsp sea salt

½ tsp ground pepper

2 (1½ lbs [680 g]) **chicken breasts**, flattened and sliced into strips

2 **eggs** whisked

Preheat your oven to 350°F (176°C).

Start by lining a baking sheet with aluminum foil. Arrange bacon strips by laying them out flat on the sheet. Put in oven and bake for 20 minutes or until bacon is crispy. Reserve the fat.

Using tongs, remove the slices of bacon from pan and set aside on a plate to cool. Once slightly cooled, put bacon slices into a small food processor and pulse until you reach a granular consistency. Pour ground bacon into a separate glass bowl and add in almond flour and desired spices to create the complete "crust" mixture.

Meanwhile, cover chicken breast in plastic wrap and flatten using a metal meat mallet. Cut them into 1 inch (2½ cm) strips. Whisk eggs in a small glass bowl. In a large cast-iron skillet, add in some leftover bacon fat and heat on medium to high. Take each chicken strip and dip gently in egg wash and then roll in the "crust" mixture to coat evenly while pressing it in and covering with your hands. When cooking oil is hot, arrange "breaded" strips in the frying pan and cook for about 3 minutes or so on each side. Using tongs, flip when side looks crispy and repeat on other side. Do not turn too early, be patient. Keep a close eye, as you do not want to overcook! When cooked, allow them to cool and continue crisping on wire rack.

+ **NUTRIENT DENSITY FACT:** Bacon is an excellent source of phosphorus and has over 1x the RDA for selenium. Bacon is also a very good source of vitamins B_1, B_3 and B_{12} and is a good source of zinc.

SLOW & STEADY SPICED PORK SHOULDER

Don't you just love those meals that you can throw in the slow-cooker and forget about until the cooking time is up? This is one of those dishes that definitely qualifies as a "set it and forget it" kind of deal. You can put it on before you leave for work and come home to an awesome aroma as soon as you walk through that door. If that isn't your speed, toss it in the slow cooker on a weekend around noon and let it cook away while you get other things done. You don't have to check it (resist lifting the lid, as this will add to your total cooking time) and just let it braise. Before you know it, you will be left with tender meat that will shred so nicely with the touch of a fork. Tastes terrific on its own or feel free to serve the pulled pork on lettuce leaves topped with fresh salsa and guacamole, or change things up a bit with some diced up fresh peaches when they are in season! Yum!

MAKES 4 SERVINGS

3 to 4 lb (1.4 to 1.8 kg) **pork shoulder**, boneless

10 **fresh garlic** cloves, halved

generous amount sea salt and ground pepper

1 (3⅓ cups [796 mL]) can **diced tomatoes**

1 cup (240 mL) **beef broth**

1 tsp black peppercorns

1 tbsp (7 g) ground chipotle powder

1 tsp ground cumin

½ tbsp (3 g) chili powder

Start by making tiny slits in your pork shoulder with a small sharp knife. Using your hands, stuff these slits with garlic cloves. Rub with a generous amount of sea salt and ground pepper.

Place pork shoulder in slow cooker and add in diced tomatoes, broth and peppercorns. Turn on the slow cooker to the high setting and let cook for 4 to 6 hours or on low for 8 to 10 hours. When cooking time is complete, remove meat from slow cooker and let sit on a cutting board.

Go back to your slow cooker and remove all the liquid and tomatoes by pouring it into a large glass measuring cup. Using a fork, shred the pork completely into long strands. Transfer shredded pork back into the slow cooker, add in spices and about 1½ cups of the liquid you just poured out, plus all of the cooked tomatoes. Do so using a slotted spoon. Stir and mix thoroughly. Turn the setting on the slow cooker to warm and the pork can be served directly from there when you are ready!

+ NUTRIENT DENSITY FACTS:

+ Pork shoulder is an excellent source of selenium. It is also a good source of phosphorus, zinc, vitamins B_2, B_5, B_6 and B_{12}. In addition, pork shoulder also contains some choline.

+ Cumin seeds are a nutrient powerhouse. They are an excellent source of calcium, copper, magnesium and manganese with over 8x the RDA for iron, as well as a very good source of phosphorus, potassium, zinc, vitamins B2 and B6.

DUCK FAT CABBAGE WITH PORK & CARAWAY SEEDS

This is a single pan dish that simply speaks volumes. Preparation wise, you would think, "Hey, this is a cinch." But the plated end product makes you feels so much more accomplished. When cooked all together, these ingredients are given time to fuse and form an amalgamation of silky rightness. Duck fat makes the big difference here. Be sure to use it! Pick up a container at your local farmers market or butcher shop.

MAKES 4 SERVINGS

1 lb (454 g) **ground pork**

3 tbsp (42 g) duck fat

1 large **red onion**, thinly sliced

1 medium **green cabbage**, chopped into 1" (2½ cm) slices

2 tsp (6 g) caraway seeds

3 tbsp (45 g) **grainy mustard**

sea salt and ground pepper to taste

In a large cast-iron skillet, brown the ground pork over medium heat for about 10 minutes. When cooked, scoop out using a large slotted spoon and set aside in a medium glass bowl.

Continue by adding in and melting the duck fat. Next, add in red onion and sauté for 10 minutes until softened and slightly browned. Add in green cabbage and cook for 10 more minutes until softened.

Pour the ground pork back into the skillet and combine everything together. Finally, add in caraway seeds, grainy mustard, salt and pepper. Continue to stir, making sure all ingredients are mixed thoroughly. Cook on low heat for another 5 to 10 minutes and then serve.

+ NUTRIENT DENSITY FACTS:

+ It is interesting to note that caraway seeds are a good source of vitamin E and have some choline.

+ Cabbage is a very good source of vitamin K and vitamin C.

MUSTARD-CRUSTED SALMON

This dish is effortless, painless and a total breeze to make if you are pressed for time!
A brisk 20 minutes in the kitchen from start to finish and this one is in the books. Splurge if you
can and pick up a high-quality grainy mustard, as this will allow the dish to reach its full potential.
If you prefer a top layer that has even more of a "crust" to it, try adjusting the cooking times and
doing so with a longer, slower broil. Please note, you must be a super spy,
and keep a close eye so it doesn't burn!

MAKES 4 SERVINGS

4 tbsp (60 g) **grainy mustard**

1 **shallot**, fined chopped

2 tbsp (30 mL) freshly
squeezed **lemon juice**

4 (½ lb [227 g]) **salmon
fillets**

2 tbsp (30 mL) olive oil

sea salt and ground pepper
to coat fillet

Preheat oven to 400°F (204°C).

In a small glass bowl, combine grainy mustard, shallot and lemon juice. Mix together
thoroughly by hand, using a whisk.

Take a silicone brush and coat the skin-side of the fillet with some olive oil so that it
won't stick to the pan. Once again, using your silicone brush, coat the top of the salmon
with the mustard mixture. Bake the salmon on a parchment-lined baking sheet for 10
minutes and then broil it for an additional 5 minutes or so, keeping a close eye on it.
Plate and serve.

+ **NUTRIENT DENSITY FACT:** Salmon is an excellent source of vitamin D and B_{12}
(approximately 2x the RDA). It is also a very good source of selenium,
vitamin B_6 and a good source of phosphorus and vitamin B_3.

PAN-FRIED CHICKEN LIVERS WITH PORK LARDONS

Organ meats are one of the most nutrient dense foods that you can include in your diet. They are packed with a variety of nutrients such as iron, zinc and B vitamins, which offer many healing properties to the body. Eating organ meat doesn't have to be intimidating, as this dish offers an easy and inviting way to introduce them to your family. Chicken livers are a great starting place if you are new or just beginning to incorporate organ meats into your weekly meals because they are quick, easy and not overpowering in the slightest. Drizzling this dish with a balsamic reduction, alongside the pork lardons, gives you that zing to signify a match made in heaven.

MAKES 2 TO 4 SERVINGS

1-2 small packages (½ lb [227 g]) **pork lardons**

1 medium **yellow onion**, thinly sliced

8 to 12 **chicken livers**, rinsed and patted dry

1 cup (235 mL) balsamic reduction (page 206)

½ cup (20 g) **fresh parsley**, finely chopped

½ tsp sea salt

1 tsp ground pepper

Begin by cooking the pork lardons on medium heat in a large cast-iron skillet. Once they have been cooking for 10 minutes, add in the onion and continue to cook and stir together for another 10 minutes or so.

Add in the chicken livers and cook over medium to high heat for about 5 minutes a side, while turning with tongs. Cook on the second side for the same amount of time. Once cooked, divide and plate the livers. Top with a heaping spoonful of the onion and pork mixture.

Prepare the balsamic reduction and drizzle on the dish. Complete each plate by sprinkling on some freshly chopped parsley. Season with salt and pepper.

+ SIDE NOTE: Use a good quality balsamic vinegar for the reduction. If you have extra, it will keep well if stored in a small, airtight glass container.

+ NUTRIENT DENSITY FACT: Chicken livers are an excellent source of iron, vitamins B_6, B_3, B_5 and B_9. They're extremely rich in vitamin A (4x the RDA) and in vitamin B_{12} (8x the RDA). They are also a very good source of copper, phosphorus, vitamin B_6 and choline, as well as a good source of zinc.

MARINATED AND BAKED CHICKEN THIGHS—3 WAYS

Today is your lucky day: three recipes, and three different ways to marinate and prepare chicken thighs, and all are equally delicious. This is an affordable way to feed your family that doesn't compromise quality and taste. Each marinade will leave you with an end product that is very different. Have fun playing around and experimenting with these—choose your own adventure! Often overshadowed by chicken breasts, give the thighs the credit they deserve and pick some up today! We based each marinade on 4 chicken thighs, but feel free to double or triple the batch if you are making just one of the marinades for all of your thighs.

MAKES 4 TO 6 SERVINGS

BALSAMIC

3 tbsp (45 mL) olive oil

4 tbsp (60 mL) balsamic vinegar

1 large **shallot**, finely chopped

2 **fresh garlic** cloves, minced

2 tbsp (30 g) **grainy mustard**

sea salt and ground pepper to taste

4 **chicken thighs**, (½ lb [227 g]) boneless

LEMON

2 tbsp (30 mL) olive oil

3 tbsp (45 mL) freshly squeezed **lemon juice**

3 tbsp (9 g) Italian seasoning (oregano, marjoram, thyme, rosemary, basil and sage)

2 **fresh garlic** cloves, minced

¼ cup (60 mL) **chicken broth**

sea salt and ground pepper to taste

4 **chicken thighs**, (½ lb [227 g]) boneless

SMOKEY

1 tbsp (15 mL) olive oil

¼ cup (60 mL) freshly squeezed **lime juice**

2 **fresh garlic** cloves, minced

3 **chipotle peppers in adobo,** finely chopped

sea salt and ground pepper to taste

4 **chicken thighs**, (½ lb [227 g]) boneless

(continued)

For each individual marinade, measure and pour all ingredients into a large re-sealable bag or casserole dish. Add in the chicken thighs and zip the bag closed. Use your hands to shake and massage the marinade mixture into the flesh of the chicken. Allow time for the chicken thighs to soak and absorb all the flavors—at least 30 minutes.

When ready, preheat oven to 350°F (176°C).

Remove chicken thighs from bag and place in an oven-proof casserole dish or baking sheet, making sure they are spaced out accordingly. Top by spooning out any extra marinade sauce over the chicken thighs.

Bake for approximately 30 to 40 minutes until juices run clear. Watch them, as you don't want them to overcook and dry out. Broil for an additional 3 to 5 minutes if you want the outside crispy.

+ **SIDE NOTE:** These are wonderful because you can marinate a big batch the night before and let them sit in the fridge overnight. This allows all the flavors to penetrate the poultry and make them even more tender. This recipe also works well on boneless, skinless or skin-on thigh, depending on your preference.

APPLE AND CABBAGE COLESLAW WITH DRIED TART CHERRIES

This juicy and tangy side is a crisp, invigorating way to enjoy a spin on your traditional coleslaw. The aromatic juices of the apple and lemon are beautifully taken in by the dried cherries. Using a mandolin slicer with a julienne attachment will help to whip up a balanced and equivalent texture that will be pleasing to the eye, and more importantly ravishingly delicious. Can't find dried cherries? No worries, other dried fruit such as cranberries, raisins or plums can be substituted here.

MAKES 4 TO 6 SERVINGS

4 **green apples,** julienne sliced (we used Granny Smith)

½ large **red cabbage,** shredded

3 tbsp (45 mL) freshly squeezed **lemon juice**

1 tbsp (15 mL) olive oil

½ tsp sea salt

1 tbsp (15 mL) balsamic vinegar (optional)

1 cup (75 g) tart **dried cherries**

Into a large glass bowl, slice your apples into matchsticks. We used a julienne slicer here to make the process easier. Slice up your cabbage with a mandolin slicer, as it will naturally become shredded, and add it into the same bowl.

Pour in lemon juice, olive oil, salt and vinegar (optional). Using your hands or tongs, toss it together so that everything is mixed well. Finally, add in the cherries and continue tossing. Let cool in refrigerator for at least 1 hour and serve.

If you tolerate dairy, add in goat cheese.

+ **SIDE NOTE:** Refrigerating and letting the coleslaw sit allows all the flavors to meld together nicely. The lemon juice also adds a nice zing and will help the apples from turning brown. If you wish, add in a splash of balsamic vinegar.

+ **NUTRIENT DENSITY FACT:** Red cabbage is a very good source of vitamin C and a good source of vitamin B_6 and vitamin K.

SWEET POTATO AND YAM CRUSTED SPINACH AND CHORIZO QUICHE

Having company over for brunch? This sweet potato and yam crusted quiche is an alluring option that your guests will appreciate. It's super straightforward and holds a uniqueness as something a little different than the common fritatta. Another bonus is that it keeps well for leftovers for the next day! Make it your own by adding in any other items you may have in the fridge. The sweetness of the crust paired with the hotness of the chorizo is a tasty union.

MAKES 4 TO 6 SERVINGS

2 large **chorizo sausages**, coined

4 large **sweet potatoes** or **yams** (or a mix of both), peeled and shredded

10 **eggs** total (2 eggs for binding and 8 eggs to whisk for frittata)

1 tbsp (14 g) cooking fat (we used duck fat)

1 cup (240 mL) water

2 cups (60 g) **spinach,** coarsely chopped

½ tsp sea salt

2 tsp (5 g) ground pepper

freshly chopped basil, for garnish

Preheat oven to 350°F (176°C).

Coin the chorizo sausage and cook over medium heat for 10 to 15 minutes in a skillet. Use tongs to turn them over until they are slightly brown on both sides. Drain excess fat if needed.

Grate the sweet potatoes and yams into a large glass bowl. We used the food processor here, but you could also use a stand grater—it would just take longer! Crack and whisk 2 eggs in a small glass bowl and then combine them with the sweet potato. Using your hands, mix everything together and create a paste-like consistency.

Grease a heavy deep (non-stick oven-safe) skillet with duck fat, making sure it is coated well. Take the potato/yam mixture and press it into the bottom and sides of pan, creating a crust-like layer. You don't want it too thick here, but you want it so there are no large gaps or holes in the crust. Bake the crust in oven for approximately 35 to 40 minutes or until edges become slightly brown. Remove and set aside and turn oven temperature up to 375°F (190°C).

While the crust is in the oven baking, create frittata mixture by whisking the remaining eggs together in a medium glass bowl. Add in water and continue to whisk. Finally, add in the spinach, salt and pepper.

Layer the cooked sausage coins on top of the crust first and then pour the egg mixture into the rest of the skillet (do not overflow). Bake in oven for 35 to 40 minutes or until middle of egg in skillet is no longer liquid. You can check with a wooden pick. Remove from oven and let cool for 10-15 minutes before slicing. Garnish with a handful of freshly chopped basil.

If you tolerate dairy add in feta, Gruyere, Havarti, mozzarella or Parmesan cheese

+NUTRIENT DENSITY FACT: Chorizo is an excellent source of vitamin B_{12} and a very good source of vitamin B_1. It is also a good source of selenium, zinc, vitamin B_3 and B_6.

SAGE-INFUSED MUSTARD AND ONION PORK CHOPS

My husband is the sole creator of this dish. In this recipe, he offers an easy-as-pie weeknight dinner selection that is smothered in a stunning, savory sauce! The use of pork lard in this meal is fundamental, as it lends to that lushness that helps make up the onion topping. Fresh sage is where it's at! These flavorsome leaves harvest a delicious flavor when coupled with the pork chops. Totally painless, have at it and give it a go!

MAKES 4 SERVINGS

3 tbsp (34 g) cooking fat, divided (we used pork lard)

8 leaves **fresh sage**, finely chopped

4 **pork chops** (1½ lbs [680 g])

1 large **yellow onion**, sliced lengthwise in long pieces

1 cup (240 mL) apple cider vinegar

2 tbsp (30 g) **Dijon mustard**

Melt 1 tablespoon (11 g) cooking fat in a large cast-iron skillet over medium to high heat. Add in the fresh sage and mix around, using a large silicone spoon. Next, place the pork chops in the skillet and pan-fry on one side for 5 minutes and then on the other side for the same amount of time, maybe even a little less. You do not want to overcook them!

In the meantime, in a separate skillet, saute onion in remaining cooking fat for 10 minutes, until softened and slightly browned. When pork chops are done, remove from pan. Set aside for 5 minutes, covering with aluminum foil.

Pour apple cider vinegar into the cast-iron pan (the one that the pork chops were frying in) to deglaze and remove all the cooked bits that are stuck to the bottom of the skillet. Use a large silicone spoon to do this.

Transfer in your cooked onion and add in the mustard, mixing well until the toppings are smooth and creamy. Plate pork chops and cover with the onion-mustard mixture, distributing evenly.

SALMON, EGGS AND ASPARAGUS OVER BUTTERY BIBB LETTUCE

Pondering what to serve as an awesome brunch? Look no further than this light and effortless meal that's simply lush. The amalgamation of Bibb lettuce, roasted asparagus, smoked salmon and runny eggs puts together a team of ambrosial ingredients that are silken to the tongue. Eggs can also be poached, but strongly consider keeping the yolks fluid as this cascade adds to the dish. Finish this plate with a few splashes of hot sauce to bring it home.

MAKES 4 SERVINGS

2 bunches **asparagus** spears, ends removed

2 tbsp (30 mL) olive oil

½ tsp sea salt

¼ tsp ground pepper

2 small heads **Bibb lettuce**, coarsely chopped

4 **eggs**

6 cups (1.4 L) water

1 to 2 tbsp (15 to 30 mL) apple cider vinegar

16 slices **smoked salmon**

Classic Sexton Balsamic Vinaigrette (page 198)

hot pepper sauce for garnish

Preheat oven to 300°F (148°C).

Line a baking sheet with parchment paper or aluminum foil and lay the asparagus on top in a single layer. Drizzle with olive oil and sprinkle with salt and pepper. Roast them in the oven for 20 minutes, or until spears are cooked to your liking. Use tongs to turn them midway through the cooking process.

In the meantime, chop the lettuce and wash using a salad spinner. Set aside.

With about 10 minutes left in the asparagus cooking time, bring the water to a rumbling boil and add in the apple cider vinegar. Once ready, place each egg in a small coffee mug and gently place mug into the hot water. Then, gently ease the egg into the water and cook for 5 minutes or until the egg whites have solidified. Use a slotted spoon to remove the eggs. Pat the eggs dry of any excess water with a paper towel and put aside.

On each plate, start with laying down a bed of the lettuce followed by the asparagus spears. Next, layer your pieces of smoked salmon and top with the egg. Drizzle with desired amount of dressing. Garnish with a few splashes of hot pepper sauce.

If you tolerate dairy, add in some Parmesan cheese.

+ NUTRIENT DENSITY FACT: Bibb lettuce is an excellent source of vitamin K.

PAN-FRIED SOLE WITH MUSHROOM AND TARRAGON SAUCE

Introducing a light and flavorful meal that is assured to amuse your appetite. Sole fillets are an economical fish option and they're perfect for someone who doesn't enjoy a strong tasting fish. Paired with a mushroom and tarragon sauce, this combo is truly irresistible. We may or may not have licked the plate clean after this one! Its luscious, creamy qualities will make this dish one to remember.

MAKES 4 SERVINGS

4 tbsp (57 g) cooking fat, divided (we used butter)

2 **shallots**, coarsely chopped

2 (2½ cups [228 g]) packages of **mini bella mushrooms**, coarsely chopped

2 tbsp (4 g) **fresh tarragon**, finely chopped

8 small **sole** fillets (1½ lbs [68 g])

sea salt and pepper to taste

In a large, non-stick skillet, melt half the cooking fat over medium to high heat. Stir in the shallots and cook for 10 minutes, or until softened. Add in the mushrooms and tarragon and continue to cook together for another 10 to 15 minutes. Reduce the heat to low and let simmer to keep sauce warm.

In the meantime, sprinkle the fish with some salt and pepper. In a separate skillet, melt the other half of the cooking fat over medium to high heat. When skillet is hot, pan-sear the sole fillets for about 2 minutes per side, turning carefully with lifter. Plate and top with a couple spoonfuls of the mushroom tarragon sauce.

+ **SIDE NOTE:** When turning the fish over, use a very thin lifter so that the fillet stays intact as they can be quite delicate. Remember! These don't take very long to cook—it is pretty much a flash fry!

+ **NUTRIENT DENSITY FACT:** Sole is a very good source for selenium and vitamin B_{12}, as well as a good source of phosphorus.

MUSHROOM AND SAUSAGE BEEF ROLL

You know those cake-y, icy, creamy chocolate and vanilla rolls you used to (or maybe still do) buy at the grocery store? The log variety type? Somehow, this shape reminds me of that but couldn't be any further from that in reality. This dish is a protein-packed cylinder, an all-in-one baby that's stuffed with spicy sausage and silky mushrooms that have been fried in coconut oil. Enjoy cooking along with your favorite choice of herbs. This is an economical choice that will feed a large number of people.

MAKES 6+ SERVINGS

3 tbsp (42 g) cooking fat (we used coconut oil)

2 (2½ cups [228 g]) packages **cremini mushrooms,** chopped

6 large **sausages** of choice, casing removed—a spicy variety is preferred

1½ to 2 lbs (680 g to 908 g) **beef eye of round,** butterflied and tenderized

3 sprigs of **fresh rosemary,** or other **fresh herbs**

sea salt and pepper to season

Preheat oven to 350°F (176°C).

In a large skillet on the stovetop, begin by melting the cooking fat over medium heat. Start by cooking and stirring your mushrooms for 10 to 15 minutes, until slightly softened.

Remove the outer casing from the sausage, leaving the meat from the inside. Place this in a large glass bowl and set aside. On a cutting board, flatten out the beef by using a heavy steel tenderizer to pound the meat on both sides, using the pronged side of mallet.

Using your hands, take the meat from the sausage and spread a thin even layer on top of the eye of round. Leave about 1 inch (2.5 cm) of free space around the entire perimeter. Following that, take your slightly sautéed mushrooms and layer on top of the sausage.

Carefully roll the entire ensemble until the opening edges meet and then overlap with that inch of extra spacing. Using some butcher twine, secure the roll by tying off tight knotted sections, spacing them a couple inches apart, until the entire log has been bound. As a finishing touch, tuck in fresh herbs of your choice on top and underneath the strings for added flavor.

Season the meat with some salt and pepper and place it on a wire-racked baking sheet. Place in oven and bake for 40 to 45 minutes. Remove and let sit for at least 15 minutes before slicing.

+ **SIDE NOTE:** Cut slices so that they are about 1 inch (2.5 cm) thick and lay on plate in a wheel-like fashion. When doing so, leave the butcher's twine on there as this will help to keep it together! Ensure layer of sausage meat is not too thick, or it will not cook through.

+ **NUTRIENT DENSITY FACT:** Baby bella mushrooms are a good source of copper, selenium and vitamins B_3 and B_5. This is unusual, as selenium is not found in many foods other than meats and seafood.

BUTTERY LAMB CHOPS INFUSED WITH MINT AND LEMON

Once plated and served, this dish will honestly leave you and your dinner guests thinking that they are at some sort of high-end restaurant. Having said that, the cooking process really couldn't be any easier. Searing the lamb in a cast-iron skillet allows all the juices to stay within the meat. Creating your own herbed butter makes for an elegant way of finishing off the dish under the broiler. These bone-in loin chops are so delectable that you are going to want to make sure you get every little bit off that bone!

MAKES 2 SERVINGS

⅓ cup (76 g) unsalted butter, softened at room temperature

zest from **1 small lemon**

2 cloves **fresh garlic,** minced

½ tbsp (1¼ g) **fresh mint** leaves

4 **lamb loin chops** (1 lb [454 g])

½ tsp sea salt

½ tsp ground white pepper (if not, use black pepper)

1 tbsp (14 g) cooking fat (we used butter)

Start by creating your herbed butter. To do this, combine butter, lemon zest, garlic and mint leaves in a small food process. Pulse for 15 seconds or until everything comes together in a creamy consistency. Using a spoon, remove from food processor and put into a small ramekin or bowl and set aside for later.

Season loin chops generously with salt and white pepper. In a heavy cast-iron skillet (oven safe), melt cooking fat on medium to high heat until sizzling. Gently place chops in skillet, so that they are not touching one another. Allow time to sear undisturbed for 4 minutes. After one side has been seared, flip them over using a pair of tongs and sear for an additional 4 minutes on the other side.

At the same time, set your oven to broil and let heat up. Place a dollop of herbed butter on each loin chop, using a melon baller or small spoon. Place entire skillet on the middle rack and broil for 1½ minutes or until butter has melted, or you can plate and serve as is.

+ NUTRIENT DENSITY FACTS:

+ Lamb loin chops are an excellent source of vitamin B_{12}. They are very good source of selenium and a good source of iron, zinc and vitamin B_3.

+ Fresh mint is an excellent source of iron and a good source of manganese, copper and vitamin B_9.

ZUCCHINI, FENNEL AND SARDINES IN MARINARA SAUCE

As many of you know, I love sardines. I adore them any time of the day, with nothing, on whatever, by themselves or tucked away shyly in a dish. If you want to sneak these nutrient dense beasts into your meal in a buried and beautifully concealed way, then this recipe has you covered. I've got your back! I get it, sometimes folks need a gentle(ish) way of introducing certain foods into their repertoire. This brew of ingredients is a mingling that guides you on your path into becoming a full-blown sardine advocate.

MAKES 4 SERVINGS

2 tbsp (28 g) cooking fat (we used coconut oil)

5 medium **zucchini**, cubed

1 whole **fennel bulb**, sliced

1 (5½ cups [720 g]) jar **marinara sauce**, store bought

4 tins **wild sardines**, drained (1 cup [80 g]) and halved

1 tsp sea salt

½ tsp ground pepper

In a large cast-iron skillet, melt cooking fat over medium heat. Add in zucchini and sauté for 15 minutes until softened, stirring occasionally. Next, stir in the fennel and cook for another 10 to 15 minutes.

Add in the marinara sauce and continue to cook on low to medium heat for another 5 minutes. In the meantime, drain and remove the sardines from the tins and cut them in half. Stir in the sardines into the rest of the skillet over low heat. Season with salt and pepper.

+ SIDE NOTE: Look for a minimal ingredient marinara sauce—the one we use contains vine ripe plum tomatoes, tomato puree, extra virgin olive oil, garlic, sea salt, parsley, basil, oregano, black pepper and citric acid (naturally derived). Or better yet, feel free to make your own homemade sauce. When buying your sardines for this recipe, go for good quality ones packed in water and sea salt—no extra business necessary!

BALSAMIC AND FIG PORK TENDERLOIN

Well hello there, beautiful! This charming creation is nothing short of grand. These ingredients conspire together to construct a feast that will appease your senses. When cooked in this manner, you are left with a hunk of meat that is the exact opposite of dry. A meat thermometer is the gold star here, as it ensures that your tenderloin is cooked to excellence. The aromatic nature of the fresh rosemary completes this dish and works in harmony with the sweet, honey tasting figs and balsamic.

MAKES 4 TO 6 SERVINGS

1½ to 2 lbs (680 g to 908 g) **pork tenderloin**

2½ tsp (12 g) sea salt

¼ cup (56 g) pork lard, divided

¼ cup (60 mL) to ½ cup (120 mL) balsamic vinegar

3 medium **yellow onions**, sliced lengthwise

3 sprigs **fresh rosemary**

8 **fresh figs**, quartered

Preheat oven to 400°F (204°C).

Let meat sit for 15 to 30 minutes on a cutting board to come to room temperature. Pat dry with paper towel and season both sides generously with salt.

In a large cast-iron skillet, melt 2 tablespoons (22 g) of lard over high heat. When skillet is hot, sear each side of the meat for 2 to 3 minutes (10 to 12 total) or until golden brown on the outside.

Using tongs, transfer pork to a wire-racked roasting pan and cook for 20 to 30 minutes or until the internal temperature has reached 140°F (60°C). Check this using a meat thermometer. Remove and let sit, tented with aluminum foil for 10 minutes.

Immediately after you have removed the seared pork from the skillet, the deglazing process should follow. Reduce the heat to medium and pour in the balsamic vinegar into the cast-iron skillet. Using a silicone spatula, scrap off all the leftover cooked bits.

Add in the onion and remaining 2 tablespoons (22 g) of lard and cook and stir for 10 minutes, or until they start to soften. Drop in the rosemary sprigs and sauté for another 5 to 10 minutes. Finally add in the figs, stirring gently on low for 5 to 7 minutes. Using tongs, remove the rosemary sprigs. Cut the pork across the grain into ½ inch (1.3 cm) slices and plate. Top with balsamic, fig and onion mixture.

MAPLE CHIPOTLE GLAZED BABY BACK PORK RIBS

Holy smokes! I swear we didn't talk or come up for air the first time we made this one. This recipe is honestly one of our all time favorites. Cooking them in this fashion produces fall-off-the-bone meat that also holds the distinction of being both crispy and saucy. The other thing that is truly wonderful about this recipe is that it produces lots of extra sauce for dipping. In honor of our Canadian roots, we had to at least include one recipe with maple syrup in it. This one is tip-top!

MAKES 4 SERVINGS

FOR THE DRY RIB RUB

2 tbsp (15 g) smoked paprika

2 tsp (5 g) ground cumin

1 tbsp (8 g) chili powder

1 tbsp (7 g) cayenne pepper

2 tsp (5 g) dry mustard powder

1 tsp ground coriander

2 tsp (10 g) sea salt

½ tsp ground pepper

2 (1 lb [454 g]) racks of **baby back pork ribs**

FOR THE MAPLE CHIPOTLE GLAZE

½ cup (120 mL) **coconut aminos**

⅓ cup (80 mL) **maple syrup** (good quality)

1 (⅝ cup [156 mL]) can **tomato paste**

3 tbsp (45 mL) apple cider vinegar

2 tsp (6 g) ground chipotle

1 tsp onion powder

1 tsp garlic powder

1 tsp sea salt

Preheat oven to 325°F (162°C).

In a medium glass bowl, combine all spices and stir together to create the dry rub. Place each rack on a large cutting board and generously rub each rack on both sides, pressing in the mixture in with your hands. Pour 1 cup (237 mL) of water into the bottom of a deep baking pan. Transfer racks of ribs onto a wire rack and gently set into the pan. Bake covered with aluminum foil for 50 minutes.

Remove pan from oven and carefully transfer the wire rack with the ribs onto a baking sheet. Continue to bake uncovered and without the water for 35 minutes. In the meantime, prepare the glaze by mixing all the ingredients in a bowl. Once the ribs are done, remove and generously coat the top side of each rack with the maple chipotle glaze using a silicone brush. Bake for another 10 minutes with the sauce on.

Finish by broiling them for 2 minutes, keeping a close eye on them. Remove and let rest for 5 minutes before slicing and serving. Use additional sauce for dipping, as this recipe will yield lots of leftovers, or you can slice up ribs and toss in sauce. Extra can be stored in a container in the refrigerator.

+ **NUTRIENT DENSITY FACT:** Pork ribs are a very good source of selenium, as well as a good source of zinc, vitamins B_1, B_2, B_3, B_5, B_6 and B_{12}.

ROASTED DUCK BREAST WITH GINGERED CHERRY SAUCE

Treat yourself with this rich and delicious dish. The answer for a perfect meal to celebrate a special occasion, or better: just a way to spoil yourself and your loved ones. From the crispy skin to the savory gingered cherry sauce, this recipe will leave your taste buds dancing. Duck is at its finest when cooked medium rare, as this will lend to getting the most tender, juicy and mouthwatering morsels possible. Enjoy the wonderful combination of flavors with a side of parsnip and carrot mash (page 31).

MAKES 2 SERVINGS

2 (½ lb to ¾ lb [227 g to 340 g]) **duck breasts**, boneless and skin on

½ tsp sea salt

½ tsp ground pepper

¼ cup (60 mL) **chicken broth**

¼ cup (60 mL) raspberry balsamic vinegar

2 tbsp (28 g) **fresh ginger**

½ cup (78 g) **frozen cherries**

Rinse the duck breasts and pat dry with paper towel. Trim off any excess fat that is not needed. Using a sharp knife, gently score the duck skin in a crosshatch pattern and season both sides with salt and pepper.

Heat a large oven proof skillet over medium heat (with no added cooking fat). When hot, place the duck breasts in the pan, skin side facing down. Patience is key here, as you will let the fat render out of them to form a brown crusty layer of skin. Allow the breast to cook skin down for about 10 minutes or so. Using tongs, turn over and sear the other side for an additional 3 to 5 minutes.

In the meantime, preheat oven to 375°F (190°C). When the second side has been quickly seared, place the entire skillet in the oven on the middle rack and cook for a final 3 to 5 minutes in the pan.

Remove and let sit for 5 minutes before slicing the breasts.

While the meat is resting, use the same pan to create your sauce. Turn heat up a little bit, and pour in your broth. Using a silicone spatula, scrape the cooked bits off the bottom of the pan. Add in your raspberry balsamic vinegar and ginger, stirring continuously. Next, pour in the cherries and use a fork to mash them up a little bit. Allow sauce to thicken, while continuing to stir over medium to high heat for 10 to 15 minutes. Slice duck breasts and serve with a dollop of the gingered cherry sauce.

If you tolerate dairy, add a side of ricotta cheese.

+ NUTRIENT DENSITY FACT: Duck is a good source of copper, selenium and vitamin B_3.

SAUTÉED ENDIVE WITH SHRIMP AND RUBY RED GRAPEFRUIT

This is an interesting, complex grouping of flavor profiles that all work in concert to create an intriguing dish. Endive is quickly sautéed, which casts another attractive layer in this dish. The grapefruit and avocado are best enjoyed raw, when paired against the grilled shrimp. All the ingredients are then topped with a charming citrus dressing that just adds that last element and brings it all full circle.

MAKES 4 SERVINGS

4 **Belgian endive**, cut into long strips

3 tbsp (42 g) cooking fat, olive oil or coconut fat, divided

24 **raw tiger shrimp** (1 lb [454 g]) deveined and shelled

2 medium red/pink **grapefruit**, peeled and segmented

2 medium **avocado**, sliced

Serve with Orange Citrus Dressing (page 198)

In a medium-sized skillet, sauté the endive in 2 tablespoons (28 g) cooking fat over medium to high heat until softened and slightly browned.

While the endive is cooking, you can take your shrimp and begin the process of sautéing them in a separate skillet. Heat another tablespoon (14 g) of cooking fat over medium to high heat and place all the shrimp in the skillet. Let them cook on one side for 2 minutes and then turn them over using tongs. Allow them to quickly cook on the other side until their color has changed and they become opaque. Remove and set aside.

In the meantime or beforehand, make sure that the grapefruit has been segmented. To do this, remove the outer peeling using a small pairing knife. Slice between membranes on each side to cut out each grapefruit segment. Place these in a small bowl and squeeze leftover grapefruit juice into a mason jar. Cut avocado into thick slices and set aside.

Plate this dish by starting with a mound of endive on the bottom as the base. Next, add the slices of avocado, segments of grapefruit and finally top with the shrimp. Drizzle with citrus dressing and enjoy.

+ **NUTRIENT DENSITY FACT:** Endive is an excellent source of vitamin K and a good source of vitamin B_9.

OYSTERS WITH MIGNONETTES—3 WAYS

Oysters: a delicacy and one of the most nutrient-dense foods that this planet has to offer us! I tried my first oyster about 5 or so years ago in downtown Toronto at Rodney's Oyster House and immediately fell in love with them. Our brother-in-law's family has owned and run this establishment for over 25 years, so the inclusion of this plate was a no-brainer! Packed with iron, copper, zinc and vitamin B_{12}, a natural aphrodisiac, this healthful and beneficial creature of the sea will leave you feeling refreshed. Let mignonette ingredients marinate in the fridge to allow the flavors to come together.

EACH ONE MAKES ¼ CUP TO DRIZZLE OVER 12+ OYSTERS

SIMPLE SHALLOT

1 tsp **shallot,** minced

2 tsp (10 g) **fresh ginger,** grated

2 tsp (10 g) **fresh horseradish**, grated

¼ cup (60 mL) Sherry vinegar

½ tsp sea salt

¼ tsp ground pepper

SPICY LIME

2 tbsp (30 mL) freshly squeezed **lime juice**

1 clove **fresh garlic,** minced

1 **red chili pepper,** finely chopped

1 tbsp (15 mL) olive oil

1 tbsp (15 mL) white wine vinegar

½ tsp sea salt

¼ tsp ground pepper

CUCUMBER

1 **mini cucumber**, finely chopped

1 tbsp (15 mL) freshly squeezed **lemon juice**

1 tbsp (15 mL) **sesame oil**

2 tbsp (30 mL) red wine vinegar

½ tsp sea salt

¼ tsp ground pepper

Fresh lemon and freshly grated horeseradish for garnish

Begin by shucking the oysters (opening them) and setting them on a platter. You can do this yourself, if you know how, or you can ask the person at the seafood counter to prepare them for you at the time of purchase.

To create the mignonette, combine al ingredients in a small bowl and whisk together. When ready to eat, drizzle a small amount over the oysters using a small spoon. Garnish with fresh lemon and freshly grated horseradish.

+ NUTRIENT DENSITY FACT: Oysters are an excellent source of iron, and are especially rich in copper, zinc and vitamin B_{12}: all three of which are 6x over the RDA. Oysters are also a very good source of selenium and a good source of manganese and phosphorus.

CURRIED EGG SALAD

A staple in any brown bag lunch, this version is sure to impress. The mayonnaise is jazzed up a wee bit, with the addition of a hint of curry. This provides a really nice seasoning, which gives the end product a little extra umph. Hiding amongst the creaminess and richness of the healthful egg yolks are bits of celery that will give you that added crunch with every bite! Add this to your favorite leafy greens or simply devour it on its own. Either way, this dish will harken you back to your youth with that classic lunch that you may have once enjoyed between two slices of bread!

MAKES 2 TO 4 SERVINGS

8 **large eggs**, hardboiled and chopped

2 stalks **celery,** chopped

3 **scallions,** diced

1 tbsp (15 mL) water

1 tsp yellow curry powder

¼ cup (55 g) **Marvelous Mayonnaise** (page 206)

¼ tsp sea salt

¼ tsp ground pepper

freshly chopped chives for garnish

Place eggs in large Dutch oven and fill with cold water. On the stovetop, bring to a boil and cook for 12 minutes. Remove and drain the hot water, and refill with cold water. Let sit for 10 minutes.

Once the eggs have cooled, crack and peel off the shells. Coarsely chop up the eggs and place them in a medium-sized mixing bowl. Add in the celery and scallions. In a small glass bowl, combine water with yellow curry powder. Stir together, making sure all the clumps have dissolved.

Add this paste to the mayonnaise and stir together. Once this has been formulated, add in the curry-infused mayonnaise into the large bowl with the other ingredients. Fold together, until desired consistency has been reached and add salt and pepper. Enjoy this egg salad solo, or feel free to serve in a radicchio leaf (or lettuce of your choice). Garnish with freshly chopped chives.

+ **SIDE NOTE:** If you want your egg salad to be creamier, add in another spoonful of mayonnaise—it's totally up to you!

+ **NUTRIENT DENSITY FACT:** Although typically consumed in smaller quantities, curry powder has 3X the RDA in iron. It is also an excellent source of manganese, copper, vitamin B_6, vitamin E and vitamin K. Curry is a very good source of magnesium and a good source of calcium, phosphorus, potassium, selenium, zinc and vitamin B_9.

SHAVED ROAST BEEF SALAD WITH MARINATED ARTICHOKE HEARTS

Are you ever left wondering what to do with leftover roast beef? If so, then this recipe could be a wonderful solution. Even if leftovers aren't your thing, you can substitute and make this salad with a really good quality shaved roast beef from your favorite deli. We buy one pretty much weekly that only has the roast beef, smoke and sea salt in it. This type will also do the job, as it is a super quick and convenient way to pull together a weeknight meal. We were originally inspired to create this dish after we came up with our sun-dried tomato dressing. We wanted to tie everything together with that antipasto feel while adding in the lightness of the shaved roast beef.

MAKES 4 SERVINGS

8 cups (240 g) **mixed greens**

20 **olives,** halved

16 marinated **artichoke hearts,** halved

12 slices **roast beef**, cut into ¼" (.6 cm) strips

Serve with Sun-Dried Tomato and Basil Vinaigrette (page 202)

Kimchi on the side for garnish (store-bought)

Start by plating your desired amount of mixed greens first. Add in the olives and artichoke hearts. Top with slices of roast beef. Drizzle with sun-dried tomato and basil vinaigrette dressing and serve. Garnish with some kimchi on the side.

If you tolerate dairy, add in some bocconcini cheese.

+ SIDE NOTE: Each serving plate can be prepared separately as an individual salad, or feel free to toss everything into a large salad bowl, and serve from there.

VENISON WITH JUNIPER BERRY AND POMEGRANATE SAUCE

Venison is a very lean cut of meat; therefore, you really want to focus on cooking it to a medium-rare finish. When we sliced into this rack of venison, we were met with a pinkish, buttery meaty inside that was honestly so incredibly juicy! This dish is perfect for a special occasion, date night with your significant other or dinner with friends. It is exceedingly impressive and so easy to make. When served with a drizzle of the sauce overtop, your taste buds will experience pleasing fruity, yet piney notes that are so flattering to many game meats, especially venison.

MAKES 2 SERVINGS

4 bone **rack of venison** (1½ lbs [680 g] total)

lots of ground pepper to season meat

1 tbsp (14 g) cooking fat (we used butter/ghee)

3 cloves **fresh garlic**, minced

1 cup (240 mL) **pomegranate juice**

20 dried **juniper berries**, crushed

fresh pomegranate seeds, for garnish

Preheat oven to 400°F (204°C).

Take your rack of venison out of the refrigerator and let it come to room temperature for about 30 minutes. Season the cut with a generous amount of freshly cracked ground pepper. Place it in a roasting pan and cook for 20 minutes or until you reach an internal temperature of 125°F (51°F). Remove and set aside, tented in aluminum foil for 5 minutes before cutting into individual portions.

At the same time, with 5 minutes remaining in the roasting time, start to create your juniper and pomegranate sauce on the stovetop, so it will be ready by the time the meat has rested but is still warm. Start by heating cooking fat over medium in a large skillet or saucepan. Add in the garlic and cook and stir for 5 minutes. Pour in the pomegranate juice. Add in the juniper berries and some more ground pepper. Bring to a boil over high heat. Continue cooking the sauce at this temperature for 10 minutes, making sure you have a slight boil. During this time, the sauce will reduce and thicken.

Using a large knife, slice your venison rack into individual portion. Plate and drizzle with the juniper berry and pomegranate sauce. Garnish with fresh pomegranate seeds.

+ **SIDE NOTE:** Juniper berries may be a little tricky to find. Call around to your local specialty shops, co-ops and bulk stores to find them. The ones we used were dried and they came in a little package. It is really important to rely on your meat thermometer with this dish, as you do not want to overcook and dry the meat out!

+ **NUTRIENT DENSITY FACT:** Venison is an excellent source of vitamin B_{12}. It's also a very good source of iron, vitamin B_3 and B_6 and a good source of copper, phosphorus, zinc and vitamin B_2.

CHICKEN HEART SKEWERS WITH CHIMICHURRI SAUCE

I first tried chicken hearts when we were out for dinner at a Brazilian barbeque joint. They were so good! How could they not be? Anything on the grill rocks in my opinion. After buying some metal skewers at the market, we decided to create these sticks of nutritious organ meat ourselves. Be certain to source your hearts fresh from your local butcher shop. You may have to place an order ahead of time so that they have them in stock and ready for you. The fresher the better! Once you have them home and are ready to put them together, make sure you wash them thoroughly and clean things up. The end result is crispy, bite-size morsels that are packed with vitamins and minerals. Brazil meets Argentina when you drizzle these skewers with a little bit of chimichurri sauce.

MAKES 4 SERVINGS

FOR THE CHIMICHURRI SAUCE

1 cup (40 g) **fresh parsley**

3 tbsp (6 g) **fresh oregano**

4 cloves **fresh garlic**

⅓ cup (80 mL) olive oil

3 tbsp (45 mL) white wine vinegar

¼ tsp red pepper flakes

¼ tsp sea salt

¼ tsp ground pepper

FOR THE CHICKEN HEARTS

1 to 1½ lbs (454 to 680 g) **chicken hearts**, cleaned

1 tsp coarse sea salt

½ tsp ground pepper

3 tbsp (42 g) cooking fat (we used chicken schmaltz)

a squeeze of fresh lemon for garnish

Begin by making the chimichurri sauce first because it needs to meld together in the fridge for a few hours to overnight. To do this, combine the parsley, oregano and garlic in a small food processor and pulse until minced. Transfer by spooning it out into a medium glass bowl.

Add in the olive oil, white wine vinegar, red pepper flakes, salt and pepper. Whisk together.

Cut off the ends of the hearts to remove the ventricles then slice in half. Wash thoroughly under running water. Pat dry using a paper towel and sprinkle with salt and pepper. Assemble skewers by placing them tightly together to form a kebab. In the meantime, on a grill pan, heat cooking fat over medium to high heat. Grill each side of the skewer for 5 minutes on all four sides, rotating every 2½ minutes. Do this until the outside has become crispy. Remove from heat and drizzle with the chimichurri sauce and garnish with a squeeze of fresh lemon.

+ **SIDE NOTE:** These can be done both on an indoor grill pan or outdoors on the BBQ.

+ **NUTRIENT DENSITY FACT:** Chicken hearts have over 3x the RDA for vitamin B_{12} and are also an excellent source of iron. They are a very good source of copper, zinc, vitamin B_2 and B_5, as well as a good source of phosphorus.

LITTLENECK CLAMS WITH SHALLOT AND GARLIC BUTTER

Steaming seafood in water or your favorite broth is honestly probably one of the most accessible ways to cook these mollusks. This is a fast technique that works like a charm every time. Instead of serving with a broth, as the mussels are presented in this book, we decided to pair these clams with a butter dipping sauce infused with sweet shallots, thyme and fresh garlic for a pleasing counterpart. Once cooked, divide into bowls and drizzle with some of the butter sauce. Dip each one in some for extra flavor!

MAKES 2 TO 3 SERVINGS

2 lbs (908 g) **littleneck clams**

½ cup (114 g) butter

1 large **shallot**, minced

4 cloves **fresh garlic**, minced

2 tsp (2 g) chopped **fresh thyme**

2 cups (475 mL) water

a squeeze of fresh lemon for garnish

Start by cleaning and rinsing your clams and set aside in a medium glass bowl filled with water to remove grit. In the meantime, make your sauce by heating butter in a small saucepan over medium heat. Add in the shallots and stir and cook for 5 minutes. Then, add in the garlic and reduce heat to low-medium. Finally, add in the fresh thyme and let cook and simmer together until the clams are ready to go.

In the meantime, add water to a wok and bring to a boil. Once you have reached a boil, add in the clams and cover. Steam for 5 to 7 minutes or until all clams have opened. Discard any un-opened clams. Divide clams up into small bowls. Drizzle with some of the butter and leave the remainder for dipping. Garnish with a squeeze of fresh lemon.

+ **SIDE NOTE:** Soak these clams in water before steaming in order to remove all the grit. After steaming, be certain to discard any unopened clams as they have expired.

+ **NUTRIENT DENSITY FACT:** Clams have over 40x the RDA for vitamin B_{12}. They are also an excellent source of iron and vitamin A and a very good source of copper. Clams are a good source of magnesium, phosphorus and vitamin B_2 as well.

DOUBLE-DECKER NACHOS

This mound of goodness is honestly a heap of food that is best enjoyed with a group of people. Think Super Bowl, birthdays, get-togethers, engagements or other celebrations—this dish will most certainly be gobbled up in a flash! This baking sheet technique works well and serves up a perfect presentation that would make any partygoer proud. An awe-inspiring alternative to corn or potato chips, these taro roots are fried in a more healthful oil. If you can tolerate dairy, a good quality melted cheese will be sure to knock your socks off!

MAKES 4 + SERVINGS

1 to 2 large **taro roots**, peeled and sliced

½ cup (114 g) cooking fat (we used coconut oil)

2 lbs (908 g) **ground beef**

1½ tsp (4 g) ground chipotle peppers

½ tsp cayenne

½ tsp paprika

½ tsp sea salt

3 **jalapeño peppers**, thinly sliced

1½ cups (355 mL) **salsa**, Hot 'n' Spicy Salsa (page 194), or store bought

Freshly chopped cilantro and Creamy Garlicky Guacamole (page 197), for garnish

Using a cutting board, peel the skin from your taro root by slicing it downwards with a small, sharp knife, or peeler. After that, chop the cylinder down the middle to create a half circle shape. Using a mandolin, carefully put your chunks through and slice on the middle setting.

Melt the cooking fat in a large heavy cast-iron skillet on medium to high on the stove-top—there should always be about ¼ inch (.6 cm) of oil in the pan. If it gets low, add in some more to top it off. Cook your taro root slices in batches. Make sure that each batch is spread out into a single layer without overcrowding in the skillet. Allow the slices to fry in the oil for about 2 minutes and then use tongs to turn them over to fry the other side. Finish them off by turning them over one more time. Keep a close eye on them and turn frequently, as you do not want them to burn. You will know they are close to being done when the edges start to curl up a little bit and turn golden brown. When one batch is finished, take them out with tongs and transfer them to a wire rack to cool. Continue cooking in manageable batches until all your taro root slices have been fried.

In the meantime, cook your ground beef over medium heat in a large cast-iron skillet. Add the dried spices once it has browned. Remove and set aside in a large glass bowl. Line a large baking sheet with parchment paper or aluminum foil. Start by spreading out one layer of cooked taro chips. Next, top with half of your cooked ground beef mixture, half of the salsa and half of the jalapeño slices.

If you tolerate dairy, add in layers of shredded cheese of choice for extra goodness (totally optional). Repeat this layering process one more time so that the baking sheet is a double layer and all your ingredient have been nicely covered. Turn your oven to broil and allow a few minutes to heat up. Place the baking sheet in the oven to broil for 3 to 5 minutes so that everything has a chance to warm up together or melt the cheese (if included). Remove and scoop out servings using a silicone lifter. Top with a spoonful of salsa and guacamole. Garnish with freshly chopped cilantro.

+ **NUTRIENT DENSITY FACT:** Taro root is a good source of vitamin C.

STRIP LOIN STEAK WITH ROASTED GARLIC AND ROSEMARY BONE MARROW BUTTER

I grilled up a strip loin, but this recipe would work really well with your favorite cut of steak. You can also choose to cook your steak on the barbeque or on an indoor grill, depending on what you have access to. When marrowbones are roasted, they have a delicious bubbly center that is pretty much as decadent as it gets. Combine the creamy roasted garlic and voilà—you have a meat butter spread that will win the hearts of many carnivores.

MAKES 2 SERVINGS

2 small heads **fresh garlic**, roasted (you may not need all of this, taste test as you mix with the marrow)

2 tsp (10 mL) olive oil

sea salt and ground pepper

2 large (1½ lbs [680 g]) **marrow bones** cut into halves lengthwise/canoe-style, roasted

2 tbsp (6 g) **fresh rosemary**, minced

2 tbsp (29 g) cooking fat, divided (we used butter)

2 (.8 lb [363 g]) **New York strip loin steaks** (1" [2.5 cm] thick)

Preheat oven to 375°F (190°C).

Line a baking pan with aluminum foil. Take the heads of garlic, remove outer skin and chop off top. Drizzle them with the olive oil. Sprinkle them with some salt and pepper for seasoning. Wrap them both up in some tin foil and put into the pan. Place in oven and roast for 20 minutes, by themselves.

Add the bones to the pan to roast for a bit with the garlic. Make sure that they are marrow side up when roasting. Place back in the oven and roast both items for an additional 25 minutes at 400°F (200°C). Halfway through this part of the cooking process, briefly remove and sprinkle the rosemary onto the marrowbones. Turn off the oven but keep everything warm in there while the steak is grilling on the stovetop, grill or barbeque.

To prepare the steaks, remove from the refrigerator and bring to room temperature. Using a silicone brush, coat pan with 1 tablespoon (14 g) melted cooking fat. Right before you grill them, season with salt and pepper. Heat grill pan over medium to high heat. Once the pan is hot, gently place the steaks in there and cook on each side for 5 to 7 minutes, turning with tongs (for medium-rare). When cooked to your liking, remove from pan and let sit for 5 minutes on a cutting board.

While this is resting, scoop out the roasted bone marrow using a small spoon and place into a small glass bowl. Combine with roasted garlic cloves, add remaining cooking fat and mix together with a fork, creating a butter-like consistency. Plate steaks and top with a spoonful of the garlic, rosemary-marrow spread.

+ SIDE NOTE: You can purchase marrowbones at most local butcher shops. Ask your butcher to slice them lengthwise, canoe-style, before taking them home. This makes for easy roasting!

PEAR AND PROSCIUTTO SALAD WITH TOASTED PINE NUTS

Italian pears are honestly the bee's knees. Abate Fetel is their real varietal name. I found these gems at one of our local fruit and vegetable markets. They were highly recommended by one of the gentlemen working there as an awesome, sweet yet crisp aromatic pear. Boy oh boy, was he right! The slight bitterness of the arugula combined with the pureness and juiciness of the pear alongside the ribbons of prosciutto makes this dish a classical light, summery number! Enjoy the crunch of a few toasted pine nuts with a drizzle of honey mustard dressing to dot the i's and cross the t's! This is a tossed brew that will make you sad once it is all over!

MAKES 4 SERVINGS

½ cup (62 g) **pine nuts**, toasted

8 cups **arugula**

Honey Mustard Dressing (page 205)

4 to 6 slices of **prosciutto**, cut into ½" (1.3 cm) ribbons

1 large **pear** (we use Abate Fetel—Italian pears) thinly sliced

Begin by toasting the pine nuts in a non-stick skillet over medium heat for 10 to 15 minutes, stirring regularly. Place arugula in a large glass bowl, add in pine nuts (toasted) and drizzle with half of the dressing. Using tongs toss together, making sure that all are coated.

Plate the arugula and pine nuts mixture in salad bowls, or on individual plates. Top with pear and prosciutto slices. Once all servings have been divided, drizzle each bowl with remaining dressing.

If you tolerate dairy, add some Parmesan cheese. (Highly recommended!)

+ **NUTRIENT DENSITY FACT:** Pine nuts have approximately 3x the RDA in manganese. They are also an excellent source of copper and phosphorus, as well as a very good source of iron, magnesium, zinc, vitamins E and K and a good source of vitamins B_1 and B_3.

ROASTED CAULIFLOWER WITH RAISINS AND PINE NUTS

Roasting cauliflower is one of my favorite ways to prepare it. Cooking it in the coconut oil gives it a slight nuttiness and allows the outsides of the florets to turn into crispy little brown bits. When chopping the cauliflower, make sure that they are cut into fairly small pieces as you want them to cook evenly all the way through (even the stem, which can sometimes take longer if it is too thick). Give it a go today and switch things up a little bit. I bet that you will never go back to steamed cauliflower!

MAKES 2 TO 4 SERVINGS

1 head large **cauliflower**, cut into florets

3 tbsp (42 g) cooking fat (we used coconut oil)

¼ cup (30 g) **pine nuts**, toasted

¼ cup (38 g) **sultana raisins**

1 tbsp (15 mL) freshly squeezed **lime juice**

freshly chopped cilantro for garnish

Preheat oven to 350°F (176°C).

Coat cauliflower florets with cooking fat and place in a large, deep baking pan along with your cooking fat and roast in the oven for 30 to 35 minutes. Turn regularly until they are caramelized and browned on all sides.

In the meantime, toast your pine nuts in a small pan on the stovetop over medium heat. Cook them for 5 to 7 minutes while shifting the pan so that they are toasted evenly and slightly golden. In the last two minutes, add in the raisins in order to warm them a little.

Once the cauliflower is done, remove and plate on a platter. Top with the pine nuts and raisins. Right before serving, drizzle the entire platter with some lime juice. Garnish with freshly chopped cilantro.

If you tolerate dairy, add in some Parmesan cheese.

+ **SIDE NOTE:** A little bit of lime juice goes a long way in this recipe! You do not want it to make the cauliflower soggy. A hint is all you need! Aren't in the mood for lime juice? Try drizzling this dish with some warmed up tahini. Yum!

+ **NUTRIENT DENSITY FACT:** Raisins are a good source of copper.

SHREDDED BEEF TONGUE

My husband and I initially ate cow tongue at this really nice Japanese restaurant. I am fully up for trying pretty much anything once. Worst case scenario, if I don't like it I won't make it again. Pretty simple. When cooked properly, beef tongue is extremely tender and tasty. It basically melts in your mouth. It is fatty meat that presents itself nicely when shredded and spiced. Because I am always up for an adventure, I wanted to try making it at home—something many will never get to experience because they are simply too scared to try new things. Come on, live a little and take a stab at this one in your own kitchen. It is an amazing alternative to your usual taco filling!

MAKES 4+ SERVINGS

IN THE SLOW COOKER

1 **beef tongue**

6 cups (1.4 L) **beef broth**, homemade or store bought

2 tbsp (17 g) whole peppercorns

3 bay leaves

IN THE CAST-IRON SKILLET

2 tbsp (29 g) cooking fat (we used coconut oil)

2 medium **yellow onions**, thinly sliced

1 large **bell pepper**, thinly sliced

1 hot red pepper, thinly sliced (optional)

2 tsp (5 g) ground chipotle powder

1 tsp ground cumin

1 tsp ground smoked paprika

1 tsp ground cayenne

1 tsp onion powder

1 tsp garlic powder

sea salt and ground pepper to taste

freshly chopped cilantro or parsley for garnish

Open the package and stare at the tongue for a few minutes, just because! Place tongue in bottom of the slow cooker and pour in the broth. Next, add in the whole peppercorns and the bay leaves.

Put the lid on it and set it to cook on low heat for 8 to 10 hours. When your beef tongue has finished cooking, take a pair of tongs and remove it from the liquid and place it on a cutting board. Take a very sharp knife and cut and section off the tongue into quarters and then peel back the skin. Once you have removed and discarded ALL the skin, you are ready to start shredding the meat. Using a fork in each hand, basically start running them through the chunks of meat to pull it all apart so it resembles a stringy consistency.

In a large cast-iron skillet, heat the cooking fat over medium to high heat on the stovetop. Next, add in the onion, bell pepper and hot red pepper (optional) and cook until softened. Continue cooking on medium-high heat for a few more minutes and then add back in the shredded beef. Stir in all your spices and mix thoroughly. Finish by seasoning with some salt and pepper to taste. Garnish with some freshly chopped cilantro, or parsley.

+ **SIDE NOTE:** We enjoy serving shredded beef tongue in lettuce leaves. Radicchio cups are a fun way to present this dish, as they add color and are a perfect size. Endive works well too! Adding it to a hearty salad is always an option as well. Top with some fresh guacamole and/or salsa.

5 INGREDIENTS

This robust chapter is filled with over fifty recipes with 5 ingredients. There is variety within this chapter that will offer up something special and enchanting to every member of your family. Morning, noon or night, there is a plethora of nutritious choices that are easy enough for you to make time and time again. These recipes will fit perfectly into your weekly meal plans within your household. Switch things up a little bit with the duck egg hash. Lap up the yolks, as this is where most of the nutrients are found! Change up the game with my version of the Cobb salad. The bay scallops deal a healthful sweetness that will fuel you through the day. Finally, impress your dinner guests with the amazingly simple whole roasted trout. The browned butter will leave them coming back for more.

+ INDIAN BUTTER CHICKEN
+ CITRUS FLANK STEAK OVER MIXED GREENS
+ BURGUNDY BRAISED BEEF CHEEKS
+ HERBED BUTTERED WHOLE CHICKEN STUFFED WITH SAUERKRAUT
+ SAFFRON STEAMED MUSSELS
+ NOT-SO BORING MEATLOAF
+ DILLY TUNA SALAD
+ AKURI SCRAMBLED EGGS
+ SPICY BEEF STIR FRY WITH KELP NOODLES
+ WARM MUSHROOM AND GARLIC SALAD WITH PROSCIUTTO CRISPS
+ SWEET POTATO ALOO GOBI
+ CHUNKY BEEF CHILI
+ BEET AND BRUSSELS SPROUT SALAD
+ ROSEMARY AND LAMB POTATO PIE
+ PORK AND CRANBERRY STUFFED ACORN SQUASH
+ BACON 'N' DILL SWEET POTATO SALAD
+ PROSCIUTTO AND FIG CHICKEN ROLL UPS
+ OLIVE AND SUN-DRIED TOMATO SPAGHETTI SQUASH
+ ZUCCHINI NOODLES WITH SAUTÉED SHRIMP

+ MIXED AVOCADO, BACON AND CHICKEN BOWL
+ VELVETY ROASTED PARSNIP AND CELERY ROOT SOUP WITH CRUMBLED PANCETTA
+ PAN-SEARED SCALLOPS WITH BACON AND SPINACH
+ POTATO AND HUNGARIAN SAUSAGE HASH WITH FRIED DUCK EGG
+ THAI CHICKEN AND KELP NOODLE SOUP
+ SAUERKRAUT SALMON SALAD
+ LEMON AND TOMATO BAKED HALIBUT IN PARCHMENT POUCHES
+ MEXICAN BEEF BOWL WITH COCAO
+ ELVIS BURGER
+ SPICY STUFFED ROASTED BELL PEPPERS
+ BAKED SAGE AND PROSCIUTTO VEAL MEATBALLS
+ ORANGE-INFUSED KALE SALAD WITH CAULIFLOWER "COUSCOUS"
+ TRADITIONAL NEWFOUNDLAND JIGGS DINNER
+ POACHED SQUID SALAD
+ ROASTED TURKEY BREAST WITH APPLE-ORANGE-CRANBERRY SAUCE
+ CRAB MEAT WITH JUICY MANGO-AVOCADO SALSA

+ SPICY BRAISED OXTAIL
+ SLOW-COOKER CABBAGE AND BEEF CASSEROLE
+ COBB SALAD WITH BAY SCALLOPS
+ NIÇOISE(ISH) SALAD WITH ROASTED FINGERLINGS AND SARDINES
+ ROASTED BROCCOLI WITH GARLIC AND ANCHOVIES, TOPPED WITH TOASTED ALMONDS
+ GREEN CURRIED BUTTERNUT SQUASH SKILLET
+ LOBSTER BISQUE
+ MOROCCAN LAMB BURGERS
+ TWICE-BAKED STUFFED SWEET POTATOES
+ SANTA FE OMELET WITH SLICED AVOCADO
+ LAMB TAGINE
+ ESPRESSO AND CACAO RUBBED ROAST BEEF AU JUS
+ REALLY RED WALDORF SALAD
+ EGGS BENEDICT WITH POTATO LATKES
+ LEMON CAPER OVEN BAKED TROUT WITH FRESH DILL AND BROWNED BUTTER
+ INSIDE-OUT BISON BURGERS

INDIAN BUTTER CHICKEN

Coconut milk, oh how I love thee! You aid in making this dish so creamy, sleek and silky. This recipe is an Indian inspired dish that produces a main that consists of tender pieces of chicken drenched in a fragrant sauce that is so palatable and captivating. I always have a stash of garam masala in our cupboard because I am truly in love with this blend of spices. Mixes may vary slightly, but this combination of cinnamon, cloves, cumin seeds, cardamom and peppercorns can easily be found at many health food stores, specialty shops or online.

MAKES 4 SERVINGS

3 tbsp (42 g) cooking fat, divided (we used ghee/butter)

4 **chicken breasts** (1 lb [454 g]) cut into thick chunks

1 large **yellow onion**, chopped

½ (3¾ cups [400 mL]) can **coconut milk**

1½ tsp (4 g) **garam masala**

1 (3¼ cups [796 mL]) can **crushed tomatoes**

½ tsp sea salt

½ tsp ground pepper

freshly chopped cilantro and chopped cashews for garnish

In a large cast-iron skillet, melt 2 tablespoons (28 g) of cooking fat over medium heat. Stir in the chunks of chicken and cook. Using tongs to turn each side, cook chicken for about 15 to 20 minutes until it is no longer pink in the middle. Remove and set aside in a medium glass bowl.

Melt another tablespoon (14 g) of cooking fat in the skillet and add the onions. Cook and stir occasionally, for about 10 minutes until they are translucent and softened. Add in coconut milk, garam masala, tomatoes, salt and pepper, stirring everything. Cook together for a few minutes.

Pour in the cooked chicken and mix using a large silicone spoon. Allow all the ingredients and flavors some time to cook together. Simmer on low to medium heat for another 15 minutes or so. Plate and garnish with a sprinkle of crushed cashews and freshly chopped cilantro.

If you tolerate dairy, use heavy cream instead of the coconut milk (half the amount).

+ **NUTRIENT DENSITY FACT:** Cashews are an excellent source of vitamin B_1 and especially copper (2x the RDA). They are a very good source of iron, magnesium, phosphorus and zinc, as well as a good source of manganese and vitamin K.

CITRUS FLANK STEAK OVER MIXED GREENS

Best enjoyed when cooked on the rare side, this cut of meat will melt in your mouth after marinating in the fridge for a few hours or better yet, overnight! When you are ready to serve, it is important that you cut the meat across the grain in order to boost that tenderness factor even more. This salad screams bright sunny summer days, but relish its freshness any time of the year.

MAKES 4 SERVINGS

2 lbs (908 g) **flank steak**

½ cup (120 mL) **coconut aminos**

½ cup (120 mL) freshly squeezed **lime juice**

½ tsp sea salt

½ tsp ground pepper

1 tbsp (14 g) cooking fat, we used ghee

8 cups **mixed greens with fresh herbs**

4 **mini cucumbers**, thinly sliced lengthwise using a mandolin slicer

Orange Citrus Dressing (page 198) or Creamy Avocado-Lime Dressing (page 202)

Place flank steak in a shallow glass casserole dish. Prepare the marinade by combining coconut aminos, lime juice, salt and pepper. Whisk together and pour over the meat. Cover with a lid and let sit to marinate in fridge for 6 hours to overnight.

After marinating, remove meat from fridge. In a large heavy grill pan, melt cooking fat over high heat. When the pan is hot, lay flank steak down and sear on each side for 2 to 4 minutes depending on thickness of meat. This is best cooked and served medium-rare. Feel free to also grill this cut of meat outdoors on the barbeque.

In the meantime, prepare salad dressing of choice. Also, take the mixed greens with herbs and combine with cucumbers in a large glass bowl. Drizzle with some salad dressing and toss using tongs. When steak is done, remove and let sit on a cutting board for 10 to 15 minutes.

Using a sharp knife, cut flank steak into strips across the grain. Plate desired amount of mixed greens and sliced cucumber and top with several strips of steak. Feel free to drizzle entire dish with a little bit more salad dressing, if you wish.

> **+ SIDE NOTE:** Plan ahead when making this dish to allow time to marinate the flank steak. It really does make a difference! When searing the meat, you do not want to overcook. Try not to fiddle with it when cooking or the steak will stick to the pan! Have a look at your grocer and pick up the mixed greens that already have herbs in them.

BURGUNDY BRAISED BEEF CHEEKS

I remember a few years back when we received our first meat share farm delivery, opened up the box and saw "BEEF CHEEKS" stamped in big bold letters on one of the butcher paper packages. In talking with our farmer, he recommended preparing this very affordable cut of meat using the slow cooker. From there, this recipe was born. When cooked this way, the end result will lead you to melt-in-your-mouth goodness that is tender, succulent and flavorful. Stew-like to be exact.

MAKES 4 SERVINGS

3 tbsp (43 g) cooking fat, divided (we used duck fat)

2 large **beef cheeks** (1½ lbs [680 g])

2 large **apples** cored and cut into wedges with skin on (we used Royal Gala)

1 large **celery root** (celeriac) peeled and cubed

2 cups (460 mL) **red wine**, Burgundy or Bordeaux

4 sprigs **fresh thyme**

½ tsp sea salt

½ tsp ground pepper

In a large cast-iron skillet, melt 2 tablespoons (28 g) cooking fat over high heat. Quickly sear beef cheeks on both sides for 3 to 5 minutes each. Using tongs, remove from skillet and set aside by placing directly in the slow cooker.

In the same skillet, add in 1 tablespoon (14 g) of cooking fat. Pour in the apples and the celery root and sear for 3 to 5 minutes until slightly browned on medium to high heat. Remove from skillet using a slotted spoon and add them to the slow cooker as well, placing them around the meat.

Deglaze the pan using ½ a cup (120 mL) of red wine. Pour it in the skillet and remove the bits that are stuck to the bottom of the pan using a silicone spoon. Add this liquid into the slow cooker. Add in the remaining 1½ cups (360 mL) of red wine as well as the fresh thyme, salt and pepper. Cook on high for 4 to 6 hours in the slow cooker or on low for 8 to 10 hours. When done cooking, divide the portions of meat into your bowls and ladle with a serving of celery root and apple 'gravy' mixture.

+ **SIDE NOTE:** If you are having trouble finding beef cheeks, talk to your local farmer or butcher shop owner and they will be able to order them in advance and set some aside for you!

+ **NUTRIENT DENSITY FACT:** Fresh thyme has 2x the RDA for iron. It is also an excellent source of manganese and vitamin C. It's a very good source of copper and a good source of calcium, magnesium, vitamins B_2 and B_6.

HERB BUTTERED WHOLE CHICKEN STUFFED WITH SAUERKRAUT

Honestly, this is the best chicken I have ever tasted. Sometimes when you think
of roasted chicken, the notion of dry or overcooked can come to mind. Not with this one!
The addition of stuffing the bird with sauerkraut (thanks to my good friend, Susie), and the butter
herbed mixture works like a charm. Crispy on the outside and juicy on the inside, this roaster will
wow your dinner guests into wondering how you achieved such amazingness.

MAKES 4+ SERVINGS

1 (4 lb [1.8 kg]) **whole chicken**

¼ cup (57 g) cooking fat (we used butter)

1 tsp chopped **fresh rosemary**

1 tsp chopped **fresh thyme**

1 clove **fresh garlic**, minced

1 cup (142 g) **raw sauerkraut**

lots of sea salt and ground pepper

a squeeze of fresh lemon for garnish

Preheat oven to 400°F (204°C).

Take chicken out of fridge and rinse under cold water. Pat dry with paper towel. Let it sit and come to room temperature.

In a small saucepan, melt the butter over low heat. In the meantime, prepare your chopped herbs. Once butter is melted, pour it into a small glass bowl and add in your herbs and garlic. Whisk together.

Place chicken on wire rack in a roasting pan. Stuff the inside cavity of the chicken with raw sauerkraut. Using a silicone brush, coat the outside of the chicken skin thoroughly with herbed butter. Make sure to get all the little crevices and add the salt and pepper. You can also brush some butter underneath the layer of skin as well if you wish.

Place in oven and roast at 400°F (204°C) for first 20 minutes. Then turn down the temperature to 350°F (176°C) and continue to cook for an additional 60 minutes. The total cooking time is 20 minutes per pound. For accuracy, check internal temperature using a meat thermometer. Once 165°F (73°C) is reached, remove and let sit for 10 minutes before serving. Garnish with freshly squeezed lemon. Carve chicken and plate!

+ **NUTRIENT DENSITY FACT:** Although typically consumed in smaller quantities, fresh rosemary is an excellent source of iron. It is also a good source of calcium, copper, manganese, vitamin C and vitamins B_6 and B_9.

SAFFRON STEAMED MUSSELS

This dish is all about smoke and mirrors. The end product is exquisite, but the process of getting there couldn't be any easier! Honestly, steamed mussels in broth is one of the most flavorful, yet simple meals you can create. I used to always order mussels when I was out for dinner at a restaurant but then realized how simple and pleasing they are to whip up right in my own kitchen. They're super satisfying and a very affordable dish that your whole family will be sure to enjoy! Have fun playing around with different types of broth while combining complementary ingredients.

MAKES 2 TO 3 SERVINGS

2 tbsp (28 g) cooking fat (we used butter)

½ **fennel bulb**, thinly sliced

5 cloves **fresh garlic**, minced

½ cup (80 mL) **dry white wine** (we used Sauvignon blanc)

1½ cups (355 mL) water

1 tsp **saffron** threads (a pinch)

¼ tsp sea salt

¼ tsp ground pepper

2 lbs (908 g) **mussels**, cleaned and de-bearded

lemon wedge, for garnish

In a large Dutch oven, heat cooking fat on the stovetop over medium heat. Begin by sautéing fennel for 10 minutes or until softened. Add in the garlic and continue to cook for another 5 minutes, stirring occasionally. Next, pour in white wine, water, saffron, salt and pepper. Cover and bring to a boil.

Once boiling, reduce heat back to medium. Pour in the mussels, cover and cook for 8 to 10 minutes. Remove lid and check to make sure mussels are done and have opened. Divide mussels into portions in bowls and ladle and cover with the liquid broth. Serve and garnish with a lemon wedge.

+ **SIDE NOTE:** Discard any mussels that are still closed, as they are no good! Instead of using wine, you can switch it up by substituting fish broth or clam juice.

+ **NUTRIENT DENSITY FACT:** Saffron is an excellent source of iron, vitamin B$_6$, and especially manganese (approximately 12x the RDA). It is also a very good source of magnesium and a good source of potassium and phosphorus.

NOT-SO BORING MEATLOAF

When talking about meatloaf, I think there are two distinct camps. You either loved it or you hated it growing up as a child! I am (and always have been) a huge fan. Years ago, I remember coming home to that smell as I walked in the door from figure skating. To this day, the familiar aroma totally warms my soul and comforts me as this was a meal my mom would make regularly. My memories of this, paired with added inspiration from one of our local butcher shops, moved me to create a version of my own. For an extra zing, try dipping this meatloaf into some of your favorite mustard!

MAKES 4 TO 6 SERVINGS

1 lb (454 g) **ground beef**

1 lb (454 g) **ground pork**

2 **beets** or **carrots**, shredded

½ package (1¼ cups [114 g]) **white mushrooms**, diced

6 slices raw **bacon**, cut into small pieces (we used kitchen scissors to do this!)

½ tsp sea salt

½ tsp ground pepper

enough cooking fat to grease the pan (we used lard)

Preheat your oven to 350°F (176°C).

In a large glass bowl, combine all ingredients. Using your hands, thoroughly fold all the ingredients together so that everything is mixed really well. Press mixture firmly into a greased loaf pan.

Bake for approximately 45 minutes. Finish off the meatloaf by broiling for 5 to 10 minutes. Watch carefully so it doesn't burn, but instead just gets crispy on the top! When done, remove from oven and set aside to cool. During the cooking process, the meatloaf will reduce in size a little bit. Use tongs to remove the meatloaf, set on a cutting board and slice.

+ SIDE NOTE: Combining the pork with the beef and bacon makes it extra moist and gives it added flavor! This also helps to bind it, so egg is not needed. You can also try substituting in other ground meats, such as lamb depending on your preference. You can also sneak in some minced liver as well for added nutrients.

DILLY TUNA SALAD

Back in our bagel eating days, we would frequent this sandwich shop at the top of the street. Week after week, we would go in and get the tuna salad on focaccia. It was owned by a husband and wife, who jokingly named us "The Tuna Family" after our repeated orders. We would ask them incessantly to spill the beans and tell us what made their recipe so darn tasty! Even after our very consistent pestering, their secret remained in the vault. Sadly, one day on one of our regular visits there, this lovely couple told us that they would be shutting up shop and moving back to their home country. This was the catalyst that drove us to experiment and invent our own version!

MAKES 4 TO 6 SERVINGS

4 (1 cup [140 g]) cans of **wild tuna**, flaked

5 **dill pickles**, diced (lacto-fermented if possible)

1 to 2 large **carrots**, peeled and coined

2 tbsp (2 g) of **fresh dill**, chopped

4 tbsp (60 mL) olive oil

2 tbsp (30 mL) balsamic vinegar

5 tbsp (78 g) **grainy mustard**

½ tsp sea salt

½ tsp ground pepper

juice of 1 lemon for garnish, freshly squeezed

Open cans of tuna and pour the contents into a large glass bowl, keeping the liquid. Using a fork, mash the tuna into flakes so that all the chunks are separated into a balanced consistency.

Add in pickles, carrots and fresh dill and mix together. Drizzle with the olive oil, balsamic vinegar, and spoon in the grainy mustard.

Once you have combined all your ingredients, mix thoroughly with a large spoon and add in salt and pepper. Let sit in the refrigerator so that all the flavors have a chance to meld together. Garnish with a squeeze of lemon juice. Serve solo, in a lettuce wrap or on top of a salad.

+ **SIDE NOTE:** If you want to bring the heat, try adding in some hot sauce!

+ **NUTRIENT DENSITY FACT:** Canned tuna has over 4x the RDA for vitamin B_{12}. It is also an excellent source of selenium and vitamin A as well as a very good source of vitamin B_3 and a good source of phosphorus and vitamin B_6.

AKURI SCRAMBLED EGGS

A couple years ago, my dear friend and coworker Jasmine made me smile by emailing me one of her favorite family recipes to try out! Akuri is a spicy egg dish commonly eaten in the Parsi culture. Jasmine had been speaking about its wicked-awesomeness at work and it sounded truly incredible. I couldn't wait to give this new little number a try. I initially made this scrambled egg concoction for dinner, and again on Monday night because my family loved it like crazy! Jokingly, we argued over who got more in their bowl. Jasmine, thank you so much for introducing us to this eggcellent dish (sorry—had to). This way of doing things is a terrific alternative to regular scrambled eggs.

MAKES 2 TO 4 SERVINGS

2 tbsp (28 g) cooking fat (we used ghee)

1 medium **white onion,** finely diced

2 to 3 medium **vine ripe tomatoes**, diced

1 **jalapeño pepper** or 2 **green chile peppers** finely chopped (remove seeds if you don't want it too hot or add more if you like it really spicy!)

2 tsp (5 g) turmeric

½ tsp sea salt

¼ tsp ground pepper

8 **eggs**, whisked

½ cup (120 mL) water

handful of **fresh cilantro**, chopped

a splash of hot pepper sauce for garnish

Start by chopping up all your veggies and herbs and have them ready to go. Meanwhile, in a large cast-iron skillet, heat your cooking fat on medium. When skillet is hot, add in diced onion and sauté for 10 to 15 minutes until translucent. Next, add in tomatoes and peppers and continue to cook and stir for about 5 minutes until everything is softened. Following this, add in turmeric and season with salt and pepper while stirring together.

In the meantime, get eggs ready by cracking and whisking them together in a medium glass bowl. Pour in water to the mixture in order to create a fluffy consistency. Turn up the heat a little and pour your whisked egg mixture into the skillet. Once eggs begin to cook, add in fresh cilantro and continue folding the eggs using a silicone lifter. Continue with this constant combining motion until eggs are scrambled to your liking. Plate and garnish with a splash of hot pepper sauce!

+ **SIDE NOTE:** Feeling extra fancy? Try adding in some minced garlic to your eggs.

+ **NUTRIENT DENSITY FACT:** Whole chicken eggs are a very good source of selenium and choline. They are also a good source of phosphorus, iron, vitamin B_2, B_5 and B_{12}. Chicken eggs also contain some vitamin D.

SPICY BEEF STIR FRY WITH KELP NOODLES

Disclaimer: NO! They don't taste fishy, I promise! It took us awhile to find the kelp noodles, because in my head I was totally picturing something else. I don't know why, but I was imagining noodles of the hard/dry pasta sort of ilk. Wrong I was! They are actually a mound of soft, curly noodles packed in water and found in the refrigerated section of your health store. When we finally confirmed their existence, we bought a couple packages to take home and experiment with. Another bonus is that they have a long fridge life. Since we tried them initially, we haven't looked back. They are now a mainstay in our regular line-up and serve as an awesome alternative if you are wanting that noodle(ish) type dish or perhaps something a little different than our good ol' faithful spaghetti squash. The most beautiful thing is that they cook up in a flash and really absorb whatever flavors you decide to pair with them.

MAKES 2 TO 4 SERVINGS

2 tbsp (28 g) cooking fat (we used coconut oil)

1 package (2¾ cups [227 g]) of **mini bella mushrooms**, stems removed and quartered or ½ head broccoli, chopped into florets

¼ tsp sea salt

¼ tsp ground pepper

1 large **bell pepper**, thinly sliced

⅓ cup (80 mL) **coconut aminos**

1 package (12 oz [340 g]) **kelp noodles**, rinsed and cut into pieces

1½ lbs (680 g) **stir-fry beef strips**

A few splashes of fish sauce for garnish (Red Boat brand)

In a large wok, heat cooking fat over medium heat on the stovetop. Add in the mushrooms or broccoli florets and cook and stir for 5 minutes while sprinkling in the salt and pepper. Add in the bell pepper and continue to sauté, covered this time for an additional 7 minutes. Pour in the coconut aminos and let simmer for 2 minutes over low to medium heat. Add in the kelp noodles. Let them cook for 5 or so minutes until softened, stirring regularly.

At the same time in a separate skillet, sauté and brown the stir-fry beef strips until they're medium-rare. Transfer the beef and add it into the other skillet with the rest of the ingredients. Mix together using a large spoon and serve. Garnish with a few splashes of Red Boat Fish Sauce.

+ **SIDE NOTE:** The brand of kelp noodles that we use is Sea Tangle Noodle Company.

+ **NUTRIENT DENSITY FACT:** Kelp is a good source of iron, magnesium and vitamin B_9.

WARM MUSHROOM AND GARLIC SALAD WITH PROSCIUTTO CRISPS

Mmmmmmm...mushrooms. If you love them, then you will definitely devour this dish. Even if you aren't a fan of mushrooms, this recipe will potentially change your mind on these wee little fungi. Loaded with intense flavors, whatever variety of mushroom you decide to include will act as a sponge and absorb the gusto of the complementary ingredients. The prosciutto crisps speak for themselves. Salty and succulent, they're the perfect match to help you put the finishing touch on this hearty salad.

MAKES 4 SERVINGS

2 tbsp (28 g) cooking fat (we used butter/ghee)

1 **red onion**, thinly sliced

2 (2¾ cups [228 g]) packages of **mini bella mushrooms** and 1 package (2 cups [170 g]) of **portabella mushrooms**

6 **fresh garlic** cloves, minced

8 slices **prosciutto**

8 cups (240 g) **baby spinach**

sea salt and ground pepper, to taste

Classic Sexton Balsamic Dressing (page 198)

Preheat oven to 300°F (148°C).

In a large cast-iron skillet, melt your cooking fat over medium to high heat. Add in onion and sauté for 10 minutes or until translucent. Next, add in mushroom and continue to cook and stir for another 10 minutes. Allow the mushroom to cook down and in this process release their juices. Following this, add in the garlic and stir regularly. Let simmer on low to medium until you are ready to plate.

In the meantime, place prosciutto slices on a baking sheet lined with aluminum foil and bake for 18 to 20 minutes or until crispy (watching carefully, as these babies can burn easily—keep checking them as you go). When done cooking, transfer them to a wire rack and let them cool for a few minutes. They will continue to get crispy during this time.

The next part is super easy. Grab a handful of the spinach greens and place them on the plate. Spoon out a topping of the mushroom mix and complete the dish by tossing a couple prosciutto crisps on the side for added crunch. Sprinkle with salt and pepper. Drizzle with my Classic Sexton Balsamic Dressing.

+ **NUTRIENT DENSITY FACT:** Raw spinach has 4x the RDA for vitamin K. It is also a very good source of vitamin A and a good source of iron, manganese, vitamins B_9 and C.

SWEET POTATO ALOO GOBI

Indian food—love it. I am very fortunate to live in a city where there are several really amazing authentic Indian restaurants that serve incredible food. But what about making it at home? After having this thought, I decided to do a little research and ultimately came up with this basic, minimal ingredient aloo gobi recipe of my own. You could also take this exact recipe and use white potatoes if you wish—it's totally up to you! This dish is guaranteed to fill your kitchen with a blended and fantastic aroma of Indian spices.

MAKES 4 SERVINGS

3 tbsp (43 g) cooking fat (we used coconut oil)

1 tbsp (6 g) cumin seeds

1 large **yellow onion**, finely chopped

2 to 3 small **tomatoes**, finely chopped

½ cup (120 mL) water

1 tsp cumin

1 tsp ground coriander

1 tsp turmeric

1 tsp cinnamon

1 tsp red chili powder

1 tsp paprika

1 tsp garlic powder

¼ tsp **garam masala**

sea salt and ground pepper to taste

1 small head **cauliflower**, chopped into florets

2 medium **sweet potatoes**, peeled and cubed

freshly squeezed lemon juice and some freshly chopped cilantro for garnish

Begin by heating the cooking fat in a heavy large Dutch oven on medium. Continue by pouring in the cumin seeds, stirring and cooking lightly. You'll want to stir them frequently using a silicone spoon so they do not burn (5 to 10 minutes). Add in your onion and tomato and cook mixture on low to medium heat until softened.

In a glass measuring cup, pour in water and add in all your dry spices. Whisk together until there are no lumps. Pour liquid spice mixture into the Dutch oven and bring to a slight boil.

Add in cauliflower and sweet potato, stirring thoroughly with a large silicone spoon in order to ensure that everything is coated in the spices. Cook, covered on medium heat for about 20 to 25 minutes. After this, take the lid off, and sprinkle with some salt and pepper. Stir gently. Let sit for 10 minutes before serving as this will allow for the sauce to thicken. Garnish with some lemon and freshly chopped cilantro.

+ SIDE NOTE: Adjust amount of water accordingly depending on how liquid-y you want it! Feel free to taste and add in additional spices, depending on preference.

CHUNKY BEEF CHILI

Well, what can I say? The first thing that comes to mind is hearty and comforting. This is a wonderful, simple dish if you are cooking for a group or looking for a meal that yields leftovers. It's great for game day as you can leave this chili simmering away on the stovetop while the flavors continue to hold hands and get better. When it comes to stews, chilis and soups, sometimes they are even better the next day. Key points here are quality beef and cutting your vegetables as chunky as possible. Both of these are important factors in giving it that terrific texture.

MAKES 4 TO 6 SERVINGS

2 lbs (908 g) **ground beef**

4 tbsp (57 g) cooking fat (we used coconut oil)

2 packages (5¼ cups [456 g]) **white mushrooms**, stems removed and quartered

3 **zucchini**, diced into large chunks

2 **red bell peppers or carrots**, coarsely chopped

1 (3¼ cups [796 mL]) can of **diced tomatoes** and 1 (3¼ cups [796 mL]) can of **crushed tomatoes**

8 tbsp (65 g) chili powder

2 tsp (5 g) ground chipotle powder

In a large cast-iron skillet, cook the ground beef on medium heat stirring occasionally for 10 to 12 minutes. Remove and set aside when slightly browned. In the meantime, in a large Dutch oven, sauté all the vegetables in cooking fat on medium heat for 10 to 15 minutes until slightly softened. Drain most of the liquid from the vegetables as you don't want the end product to be too watered down.

Take the ground beef and add it back in with the vegetables into the Dutch oven. Pour in both cans of tomatoes and stir thoroughly using a large spoon. Sprinkle in the spices while continuing to mix together. Let the entire dish cook on low to medium heat, stirring occasionally for a minimum of 20 minutes. The longer you let it simmer, the tastier it will become.

If you tolerate dairy, add some sharp cheddar cheese or Monterey jack.

+ **SIDE NOTE:** The above recipe is wonderful for dividing into smaller portions and freezing because of its initial batch size. We also enjoy using it the next day as a yummy topping on eggs or over greens. Feel free to adjust the spices as you go! A little taste testing while cooking never hurt anyone!

+ **NUTRIENT DENSITY FACT:** Although consumed in fairly small quantities, chili powder is especially high in iron and vitamin E with more than twice the RDA for both. It is also an excellent source of copper, vitamin A, B_6 and K. It is a very good source of manganese, vitamin B_2, B_3 and a good source of phosphorus, potassium, selenium, zinc, magnesium and calcium.

BEET AND BRUSSELS SPROUT SALAD

I need to preface by saying that this is one spectacular little number. It could easily pose as a main for lunch or act as a superior side dish for a larger spread. The birth of this recipe began one day while strolling the farmers market. After spotting a bushel of Brussels sprouts at a vendor's booth, and some beautiful heirloom beets at another, I decided to come up with a dish that would combine the two. Ironically, I thought of uniting one of my all-time faves, beets, with something I had (at that point) never EVER tried before, Brussels sprouts. To put this dish over the edge, I knew it would be ideal to cook up some bacon in the oven first and then roast the beets, garlic and Brussels sprouts in the fat afterward. Two words: dynamite decision. After slow roasting, everything caramelizes together to make one huge mound of goodness. It creates an earthy and nutty sauce within itself. Every bite gives you a savory crunch that will appeal to your taste buds and leave you wanting more.

MAKES 4 SERVING

1 lb (454 g) **bacon**

6 **beets**, cubed into small pieces

About 24 **Brussels sprouts**, cleaned thoroughly (these guys can be dirty!)

4 cloves **fresh garlic**, quartered

1 tbsp (4 g) dried thyme

½ tsp sea salt

¼ tsp ground pepper

½ cup (62 g) **pistachios,** once cooked, and toasted

Preheat oven to 350°F (176°C).

Arrange slices of bacon on a baking sheet lined with aluminum foil and bake for about 20 minutes in the oven until crispy. When done, remove with tongs and set aside on a plate to cool. Reserve the bacon fat for cooking the vegetables.

In a large roasting pan, add in the beets, Brussels sprouts and garlic. Drizzle with leftover bacon fat. Sprinkle with dried thyme, salt and pepper. Mix thoroughly using the tongs. Roast in the oven on the middle rack for about 45 minutes until everything has caramelized slightly.

In the meantime, toast pistachios in a small pan over medium heat on the stovetop. Transfer contents of the roasting pan to a large bowl and top with pistachios. Use tongs to toss it all together.

If you tolerate dairy, add in some goat cheese.

+ **NUTRIENT DENSITY FACTS:**
  + Brussels sprouts are an excellent source of vitamin K and C.
  + Pistachios are an excellent source of copper and vitamin B_6. They are also a very good source of iron, manganese, phosphorus, vitamin B_1 and B_5 as well as a good source of magnesium.

ROSEMARY AND LAMB POTATO PIE

This isn't a cookie cutter version of your traditional shepherd's pie. It is a snazzier rendition that has been kicked up a notch by adding in some chopped asparagus with the lamb and some shredded rainbow carrots. This same combination can also be done with mashed cauliflower, regular potatoes or pretty purple yams for a vibrant color. A light sprinkling of cayenne finishes every bite with a little pizzazz!

MAKES 6+ SERVINGS

3 large **sweet potatoes**, peeled and cubed

4 to 5 tbsp (57 to 72 g) butter, divided

2 large **yellow onions**, sliced

2 lbs (908 g) **ground lamb**

3 large rainbow **carrots**, peeled and shredded in food processor

1 bunch **asparagus**, chopped

2 tbsp (6 g) dried rosemary

1 tsp ground garlic powder

½ tsp sea salt

½ tsp ground pepper

¼ tsp ground cayenne

6 cups (1.4 L) water

Preheat oven to 400°F (204°C) about halfway through the recipe.

Place sweet potato cubes in a large Dutch oven filled with water, cover and boil over high heat on the stovetop. Cook for approximately 15 minutes, covered. To check that potatoes are done, poke with a fork to determine tenderness. When cooked, drain water and then set aside, keeping them in the Dutch oven.

In the meantime, melt 1 tablespoon (14 g) butter on medium to high heat and begin to sauté the onions for 10 to 15 minutes until they become slightly browned. Using an immersion hand blender, puree your sweet potatoes to create the creamy topping. Gently stir in the sautéed onions and add 2 more tablespoons (28 g) of cooking fat into this mixture and set aside on the stovetop on low heat.

In another skillet, brown lamb over medium heat and set aside in a large glass bowl. After the lamb has been removed, begin to sauté your carrots and asparagus in the same skillet using the leftover fat to do so. Cook and stir until slightly softened for about 5 to 10 minutes. Add in rosemary and garlic powder, salt and pepper and continue to stir and cook for another 3 minutes with another 1 tablespoon (14 g) of cooking fat. Re-add the cooked ground lamb into the skillet and mix together with the vegetables with a large spoon.

Transfer meat mixture into a 1½ quart (1.4 L) oval oven safe casserole dish and spread evenly (2 inch [5 cm] thick) as the bottom layer. Top the ground lamb with a similar-sized layer of mashed sweet potato and pack down flat using a silicone lifter. Sprinkle the top layer with cayenne pepper. Bake in the oven for 30 minutes. Remove and gently coat with a thin layer of cooking fat using a silicone brush. Finish by placing back in the oven for 5 minutes on broil in order to brown the top layer (watch carefully when doing so). Remove and set aside. Let cool for at least 20 minutes before cutting and serving.

+ SIDE NOTE: If you cut into it right away, the slices will not hold together well! Be patient!

PORK AND CRANBERRY STUFFED ACORN SQUASH

New to eating acorn squash? Well, fear not, this winter squash, also called pepper squash, is easy to spot because of its unmistakable shape. Its contour actually looks like that of an acorn. It is usually dark green in color with a patch or two of orange mixed in. We love cooking these up as all-in-one meals because they can be conveniently stuffed with your most adored ingredients. This recipe provides you with a trifecta of sweet and savory with a little added crunch!

MAKES 4 SERVINGS

2 small **acorn squash**, halved and gutted

3 tbsp (42 g) cooking fat, divided (we used coconut oil)

1 lb (454 g) **ground pork**

½ head **cauliflower**, grated into a rice like consistency

¾ cup (90 g) **dried cranberries**

¼ cup (30 g) **pecans**, toasted and chopped

1½ tbsp (2 g) dried sage

¼ tsp sea salt

¼ tsp ground pepper

Preheat oven to 350°F (176°C).

Using a large knife, carefully cut the squash in half and brush the flesh sides with 1 tablespoon (14 g) of your cooking fat. Place flesh side down on a baking sheet lined with aluminum foil and bake on the middle rack for 40 minutes or so depending on the size.

In the meantime, brown ground pork for 10 minutes on medium to high heat in a large cast-iron skillet. Once slightly browned, scoop out and set aside in a separate glass bowl. Using the same skillet, pour in your grated cauliflower along with 2 more tablespoons (28 g) of cooking fat. Let cook covered over medium heat for 10 minutes. Remove lid, give it a stir and check to see that it is cooked to your liking.

Following this, add back in the ground pork and stir in cranberries, pecans, sage and salt and pepper. Cook for another 5 minutes, stirring occasionally on low heat. Try to time the dish accordingly so that the squash is done roasting at the same time the meat mixture is ready to go. When roasting is complete, turn over squash using tongs and add in a few scoops of the meat mixture into the circular cavity of the squash. Top with a sprinkling of pecans and place back into the oven. Broil for 5 minutes in order to toast them a little bit.

If you tolerate dairy, add in some Parmesan cheese and drizzle with some browned butter.

+ **SIDE NOTE:** For browned butter drizzle, heat some butter in a saucepan until it turns light brown in color.

+ **NUTRIENT DENSITY FACT:** Pecans are an excellent source of copper and manganese (1 to 2x the RDA for both) as well as a very good source of vitamin B_1 and a good source of iron, magnesium and zinc.

BACON 'N' DILL SWEET POTATO SALAD

I was originally inspired to make this recipe from a dish that we used to order at the deli counter at the supermarket near our house. One day it dawned on me to ask the gal behind the counter what ingredients were actually in the salad. A few of the ingredients she rhymed off were less than ideal, so I decided to build something simply scrumptious that focused more on quality rather than quantity. Using minimal ingredients, I turned my attention to the essence of what foods were needed to make this incredible. I did this without fillers and added sugar. After giving this salad a complete makeover, the end product is that of pure beauty. One of my tried and true favorites! A hint of sweetness, saltiness and freshness, it will be certain to satisfy your every bite. This dish screams summer BBQ! Its versatile nature works wonderfully as a smaller side, a lunch main or a perfect post-workout meal.

MAKES 4 SERVINGS

10 slices of thick **bacon**, crumbled

4 medium **sweet potatoes**, peeled and cubed

6 cloves of **fresh garlic**, quartered

4 tbsp (4 g) **fresh dill**, finely chopped

4 tbsp (60 mL) freshly squeezed **lime juice**

3 tbsp (45 mL) olive oil

1 tbsp (15 mL) balsamic vinegar

chopped scallions and pumpkin seeds/sunflower seeds for garnish

Preheat your oven to 350°F (176°C).

On an aluminum foil lined baking sheet, arrange slices of bacon and bake for about 20 minutes in oven, until crispy. When cooked, set aside on a plate to cool. Reserve the bacon fat for roasting the vegetables afterwards.

Mix sweet potatoes, garlic and bacon fat in a large roasting pan. On the middle rack, roast this in the oven for 30 minutes or until they start to caramelize, stirring occasionally. In the meantime, chop up and prepare the dill and whisk together with the lime juice, olive oil and balsamic vinegar.

Transfer the contents of the roasting pan to a large glass bowl. Add the bacon, crumbling it as you go. Finally, drizzle with dill-lime dressing mixture and toss together thoroughly. I like to use my hands here to make sure all is coated well! Garnish with some chopped scallions and a sprinkle of pumpkin or sunflower seeds.

+ **SIDE NOTE:** This dish acts as a lovely leftover, as time allows all the ingredients to fuse together! Can be served warm or cold—it's up to you!

+ **NUTRIENT DENSITY FACT:** Although not typically consumed in large quantities, fresh dill is an excellent source of vitamin C. It is also a good source of vitamins A, B_5 and B_9.

PROSCIUTTO AND FIG CHICKEN ROLL-UPS

Have you ever been waiting in line at the market, peered down and spotted a small flat of fresh figs by the cash counter? I have many times. In my mind I always think, "Wow, these look so interesting. I should get them! Hmmmm...I wonder what I can make with them though?' Whilst in mid-thought, the cashier politely says, "Next in line." And I end up leaving fig-less. Next time you spy figs, pick some up and give this recipe a go! A sweet little treat wrapped up ever so tightly in some protein. The addition of the fig, mustard and prosciutto combo is amazing—just enough to add that zingy crunch!

MAKES 2 TO 4 SERVINGS

4 **chicken breasts** (1 lb [454 g]) flattened

8 slices of **prosciutto** (2 per piece of chicken)

½ cup (125 g) **grainy mustard** (2 tbsp [16 g] per piece of chicken)

16 **asparagus** spears, trimmed (4 per piece of chicken)

5 **fresh figs**, sliced (6 per piece of chicken)

Preheat your oven to 325°F (162°C).

Using a metal meat tenderizer, flatten your chicken by pounding it on both sides, while covered under plastic wrap. Set aside once you have done this. Organize your ingredients and take out a cutting board so that you will have a solid surface to assemble your rolls.

Start by laying down a slice of prosciutto first and then place flattened chicken on top of that as the second layer. Continue building by laying another slice of prosciutto on top of that. Then, take your grainy mustard and spread desired amount over the surface of the prosciutto layer. (Don't be shy here!) Following this, place the asparagus spears horizontally on top of that. Finish by topping it off with fig slices.

Using your hands, tightly roll everything together. Repeat above instructions for each roll. Once all your rolls have been assembled, place them in a baking dish or tray that's large enough so they are not touching one another. Bake in the oven for 30 minutes, depending on thickness of chicken. Broil for an additional 3 minutes, keeping a close watch. This is optional if you wish to crisp up the top a little bit!

If you tolerate dairy, add in some goat, Gorgonzola, Gruyere or provolone cheese.

+ **SIDE NOTE:** Don't overcook this dish or the chicken will dry out!

+ **NUTRIENT DENSITY FACT:** Asparagus is a good source of vitamin B_9 and K.

OLIVE AND SUN-DRIED TOMATO SPAGHETTI SQUASH

This fusion of flavors is a sensational blend that will bring you to the Mediterranean. The olive tapenade offers a new approach to enjoying spaghetti squash—which is a little bit different than perhaps the more familiar option of using a tomato sauce. A small amount of tapenade goes a long way in this dish, as the ingredients are quite compelling and influential on their own. Olive lovers will unite, as this dish was inspired by my husband's fondness towards kalamata olives.

MAKES 2 TO 4 SERVINGS

1 large **spaghetti squash**, halved and gutted

1 tbsp (14 g) cooking fat (we used coconut oil)

sea salt & ground pepper

4 **anchovy fillets**

1 cup (150 g) **Kalamata olives**, whole and pitted

3 **sun-dried tomatoes**

2 cloves **fresh garlic**

4 tbsp (55 mL) olive oil

a handful of freshly chopped basil for garnish

Preheat oven to 375°F (190°C).

Using a large knife, carefully cut the spaghetti squash in half and remove seeds using a spoon. You can cook these seeds and eat them too if you wish! Using a silicone brush, coat the inside flesh surface generously with your cooking fat. Sprinkle with salt and pepper.

Place flesh side down on a baking sheet lined with aluminum foil. Bake in oven for about 40 to 45 minutes. You will be able to check if it is done by turning it over with a pair of tongs and piercing with a fork. When cooked, squash should easily shred away from the flesh.

In the meantime, prepare the olive and sun-dried tomato tapenade. Place anchovy fillets, olives, sun-dried tomatoes, garlic and olive oil in a small food processor. Pulse and puree until smooth or until you have reached your desired consistency. You may need more oil if it seems too thick!

When squash is finished roasting, remove from oven using tongs. Use a large fork to remove the stringy contents of the squash and place in a large glass bowl. Pour in the tapenade. Using the tongs, continue to mix the squash and tapenade until it is completely coated. Plate desired portions and garnish with freshly chopped basil.

If you tolerate dairy, add in some Parmesan, mozzarella or goat cheese.

+ **SIDE NOTE:** Don't have anchovies? No worries, you could substitute in a couple tablespoons of capers instead! Also, be certain not to overcook the spaghetti squash, as it will turn mushy!

ZUCCHINI NOODLES WITH SAUTÉED SHRIMP

Freshness amplified: divine medley of flavors that just simply works. Merging such ingredients allows them to create a beautifully blended sauce on their own as they integrate together. Invest in a spiral slicer if you can as it is an innovative and top-notch kitchen gadget that you can use for countless dishes. Discover a convenient way to create various types of noodles with an array of vegetables.

MAKES 2 TO 3 SERVINGS

4 medium **zucchini**, made into spiraled noodles

2 tbsp (28 g) cooking fat (we used coconut oil)

6 cloves **fresh garlic**, minced

24 large **shrimp** (pre-cooked), rinsed and tails removed

2 (6 cups [908 g]) packages **grape tomatoes**, halved

⅓ cup (10 g) **fresh basil**, chopped

sea salt and ground pepper, to taste

Using a spiral slicer, transform zucchini into curly noodles and set aside in a large glass bowl. In a large wok, heat up cooking fat over low to medium heat. Begin by adding in garlic and cook for 5 minutes until softened.

Turn the heat up to medium and add in the shrimp. Cook for another 5 minutes, stirring occasionally. Add in the tomatoes and continue to stir. Let cook for 10 minutes or so.

Finally, add in the zucchini noodles along with the fresh basil and cook for about 7 minutes until noodles have softened. Sprinkle with salt and pepper. If you wish, you can garnish with some more freshly chopped basil. Use tongs to plate and serve.

If you tolerate dairy, add in some Parmesan, feta, goat or mozzarella cheese.

+ **SIDE NOTE:** This recipe turns out the best if you cook it in stages rather than putting everything in together all at once. You could also try with raw shrimp, but you would obviously want to adjust the cooking time.

+ **NUTRIENT DENSITY FACTS:**
  + Although typically consumed in smaller quantities, fresh basil is high in vitamin K with over 3x the RDA. It is also an excellent source of vitamin A. It is a very good source of manganese and a good source of iron and copper as well.
  + Shrimp is an excellent source of selenium and a very good source of vitamin B$_{12}$. It is also a good source of copper, phosphorus and choline.

MIXED AVOCADO, BACON AND CHICKEN BOWL

Presenting....a BLT without the bread! As a child I used to pick off the bread and just eat the insides of a BLT sandwich. Not much has changed. A gratifying meal in a bowl that is perfect for those days where you just don't know what to make. This bowl of yumminess will be sure to hit the spot and leave you feeling content. Bowls such as this are also effective in putting leftover roasted meats to good use. This recipe was originally inspired by a friend who sent me a photo of her lunch!

MAKES 2 TO 4 SERVINGS

12 slices of **bacon**

3 **avocados**, diced into chunks

1 package (2¼ cups [341 g]) of **tomato medley**, quartered

4 cups (560 g) **roasted chicken or turkey**, shredded

¼ cup (4 g) chopped **fresh cilantro**

3 tbsp (45 mL) olive oil

2 tbsp (30 mL) balsamic vinegar

lots of sea salt and ground pepper

freshly squeezed lemon or lime juice, for garnish

Preheat oven to 350°F (176°C).

Arrange slices of bacon on a baking sheet lined in aluminum foil and bake for about 20 minutes in oven until crispy. When done to your liking, use tongs to set aside on a plate to cool.

In the meantime, prepare avocado, tomatoes and chicken or turkey and mix together in a large glass bowl using tongs. If you do not have any leftovers, you will need to bake the chicken breasts in a large oven-safe casserole dish for about 30 minutes until cooked through.

Next, crumble in the bacon and then add the freshly chopped cilantro. Drizzle with some olive oil and balsamic vinegar. Sprinkle with salt and pepper. Again, take your tongs and use them to mix everything together thoroughly. Garnish with some freshly squeezed lemon or lime juice.

+ **SIDE NOTE:** Feeling extra fancy? Try adding in some thinly sliced red onion. You can also roast a few cloves of garlic alongside the bacon and throw that into the mix as well. A tomato medley contains a nice variety of different tomatoes together.

+ **NUTRIENT DENSITY FACT:** Avocados are a good source of vitamin B_6, B_5 and B_9. They also contain some copper, potassium, vitamins E and K.

VELVETY ROASTED PARSNIP AND CELERY ROOT SOUP WITH CRUMBLED PANCETTA

Think cold autumn or winter's eve and then imagine yourself sitting at home enjoying a comforting bowl of soup. This thick and creamy dish definitely fits that picture. It is so hearty and filling that it can stand alone as an enjoyable main that will provide you with warmth and coziness. The added bits of pancetta act as the icing on the cake so to speak, alongside its peppery finish. This batch will feed a number of folks, so take note for a family gathering or save the leftovers for the next day!

MAKES 4 TO 6 SERVINGS

3 large **parsnips**, peeled and chopped

3 medium **celery roots**, peeled and chopped

8 cloves **fresh garlic**, whole

3 tbsp (43 g) melted cooking fat (we used lard)

12 slices **pancetta**, cubed

3.5 cups (828 mL) **chicken broth**, homemade or store bought

5 cups (1.2 L) water

½ tsp ground allspice

1 tsp sea salt

¾ tsp ground pepper

Preheat oven to 350°F (176°C).

In a large glass bowl, take parsnips, celery root and garlic and mix together with your cooking fat of choice. Use your hands to toss together, making sure the vegetables are thoroughly coated with the melted cooking fat.

Transfer the mixture onto a baking sheet lined with aluminum foil, spreading it into an even layer. Roast in the oven for 40 minutes or until slightly browned and softened. Stir occasionally, ensuring that all sides have a chance to brown.

In the meantime, pan-fry pancetta in a small cast-iron skillet for about 10 minutes over medium heat. When crispy, remove and set aside on a plate. Next, spoon out roasted vegetables into a large Dutch oven on the stovetop. Pour in chicken broth, water, allspice, salt and pepper.

Using an immersion hand blender, puree all ingredients together until smooth and creamy. Heat over medium heat until warm. Sprinkle with cubed pancetta and serve.

If you tolerate dairy, add in some Parmesan cheese.

+ **NUTRIENT DENSITY FACT:** Parsnips are a good source of potassium, manganese, vitamin C and vitamins B_5 and B_9.

PAN-SEARED SCALLOPS WITH BACON AND SPINACH

Sea scallops are quite a bit larger than bay scallops. Their top surface usually measures the same in diameter to that of a toonie. (Google Canadian two dollar coin!) Bacon plus scallops are a must, but honestly feel free to add in your favorite greens here alongside the sautéed shallots and garlic. Best served immediately for finest taste and appreciation.

MAKES 2 SERVINGS

8 slices **bacon**, crumbled

2 tbsp (28 g) cooking fat

3 **shallots**, thinly sliced

4 cups (120 g) **fresh spinach** or **swiss chard**

3 cloves **fresh garlic**, minced

6 to 8 large **sea scallops**

Using a large cast iron skillet, begin by cooking the slices of bacon over medium heat. Cook for 10 to 15 minutes, until it is slightly crispy. Remove from skillet, and set aside. Crumble bacon into pieces.

At the same time, in a separate cast iron skillet, melt cooking fat over medium heat. Add in the shallots, and spinach or swiss chard and cook until softened, 5 to 10 minutes. Once these start to cook down, add in your garlic. Finally, add in bacon pieces (cooked), and cook and stir on low to medium heat, until you reach desired doneness.

Nearing the end of the process detailed above, you will want to start cooking your scallops. In the same skillet that was used to cook the bacon, turn up heat and get the bacon fat nice and hot to fry the scallops.

Place scallops carefully in the skillet, and cook on each side for 3 minutes over medium heat. Use tongs to turn, once first side is seared. You want to let them brown to a golden color. When finished, divide portions, plating the greens on the bottom and top with the scallops.

If you tolerate dairy, add in some Parmesan or asiago cheese.

+ **SIDE NOTE:** Carefully watch the scallops as you do not want to overcook them or they will become tough and rubbery. You will know the scallops are done when they are no longer translucent in the middle.

+ **NUTRIENT DENSITY FACT:** Sea scallops are an excellent source of vitamin B_{12}. They are also a very good source of phosphorus and a good source of selenium. Sea scallops contain some zinc and choline as well.

POTATO AND HUNGARIAN SAUSAGE HASH WITH FRIED DUCK EGG

Bird is the word. I mean, duck is the real word here. Duck fat and duck eggs are key to making this plate so super duper special. Where do you find such excellence you may ask? Look no further than your local farmers market or friendly butcher shop to find these prized items. You will be looking for eggs that are slightly larger than chicken eggs and a container in the refrigerated section that's literally labeled "duck fat." Yep, that's all! The beauty of duck fat is that it will transform your potatoes into the crispiest, most appetizing golden snippets. Imagine that heap of nourishment topped with the runny bright orange yolk of the duck egg trickling down...it's simply mouthwatering!

MAKES 3 SERVINGS

3 **Hungarian sausages**, sliced into coins

3 tbsp (38 g) cooking fat, divided (we used duck fat)

15 **fingerling potatoes**, quartered

3 **sweet potatoes/yams**, peeled and cubed

1 **bell pepper**, diced

3 tsp (9 g) ground chipotle

2 tsp (10 g) sea salt

1 tsp ground pepper

3 **duck eggs**

In a large cast-iron skillet, begin by cooking the Hungarian sausage coins over medium heat. Cook them on each side for about 3 to 5 minutes or until slightly browned. When done, use tongs to turn them over and brown the other side. When finished, remove and set aside.

In the meantime, prepare the potatoes. Using a separate large cast-iron skillet, melt 2 tablespoons (25 g) duck fat over medium to high heat. Mix fingerling and sweet potatoes together and cook covered for a total of 30 minutes. During the cooking process, remove lid every 5 minutes and stir thoroughly. When there are 10 minutes left of cooking time, sauté the bell pepper in a separate skillet (the one you used for sausage). If you do not wish to sautee the bell pepper in a separate skillet, toss in with the potatoes. Either way works!

Stir the sausage and bell pepper (if you haven't already) into the potato mixture and add the spices. Cook uncovered for 5 minutes. In the meantime, melt another 1 tablespoon (12 g) of duck fat and fry duck eggs over medium heat in a skillet until desired doneness. You can do this in the first skillet that you used for the Hungarian sausage. Serve by spooning out servings of potato-sausage hash and serve with egg on top.

If you tolerate dairy, add in some feta, Gruyere, mozzarella or Parmesan cheese.

+ **SIDE NOTE:** Feel free to make the following substitutions if desired: duck eggs = chicken eggs; fingerling potatoes = butternut squash, yams or other tubers and Hungarian sausage = your favorite kind of sausage.

THAI CHICKEN AND KELP NOODLE SOUP

I think I was introduced to kelp noodles and baby bok choy around the same time. During one of our weekend shopping ventures, I precisely remember stopping in at an Asian market while on the great hunt for these commodities. Once found, they were initially prepared as two separate dishes. Later I decided to combine the two to create a pared-down variant on my traditional coconut chicken soup that is found on my blog.

MAKES 2 TO 4 SERVINGS

6 cups (1.4 L) **chicken broth,** homemade or store-bought

3 cups (420 g) roasted **chicken**, shredded

1½ tbsp (25 g) **red curry paste**

2 cups (180 g) **baby bok choy**, chopped

1 (16 oz [454 g]) package **kelp noodles**, cut into smaller pieces

1 tsp sea salt

½ tsp ground pepper

freshly chopped cilantro and a squeeze of fresh lime juice for garnish

In a large Dutch oven, pour in the chicken broth and bring to a slight boil on over high heat. Reduce to medium and stir in chicken and red curry paste. Cook for 5 minutes. Add in the baby bok choy, kelp noodles and salt and pepper. Let cook for 8 to 10 minutes or until softened. Garnish with juice of a lime wedge and a handful of fresh cilantro.

+ **SIDE NOTE:** This recipe is great for using up leftover roasted chicken that you may have in the fridge. Feel free to add in any other vegetables that you wish to the soup as well!

+ **NUTRIENT DENSITY FACT:** Baby bok choy is an excellent source of vitamin K and a good source of vitamin C.

SAUERKRAUT SALMON SALAD

Want a quick, easy and satisfying lunch that is not only super nutritious but foolproof to make? Look no further and enjoy this recipe as a great option to take with you to work or to quickly eat if you are in a pinch for time! Eating this dish provides you with a good dose of omega-3 fatty acids and probiotic properties. The celery offers a craved crunch and the sauerkraut finishes this dish with a zippy probiotic zing that is most enjoyable.

MAKES 2 TO 3 SERVINGS

2 (1¼ cups [150 g]) can wild-caught **sockeye salmon**

1 cup (145 g) **sauerkraut**

2 tbsp (30 g) **grainy mustard**

2 stalks of **celery**, thinly sliced

10 **grape tomatoes**, quartered

2 tbsp (30 mL) balsamic vinegar

3 tbsp (45 mL) olive oil

¼ tsp sea salt

¼ tsp ground pepper

freshly chopped chives, a squeeze of lemon juice and avocado slices for garnish

In a medium bowl, pour in canned salmon and flake with a fork. Don't drain it—use the liquid, too! Mix in sauerkraut, grainy mustard, celery and tomatoes. Add in balsamic vinegar, olive oil, salt and pepper and continue to stir gently. Garnish with some freshly chopped chives and a squeeze of lemon juice and avocado slices. Serve on a bed of arugula or watercress. Can also be eaten as is or in a large lettuce leaf.

+ SIDE NOTE: Best when served immediately!

LEMON AND TOMATO BAKED HALIBUT IN PARCHMENT POUCHES

Halibut is a mild and tender fish that works perfectly with this steaming technique. It is so super swift that you honestly won't believe it! Pop all your ingredients into a parchment paper pouch, tuck it in the oven and the rest is history. It'll be done in a flash. In less than 15 minutes, you have yourself a very healthy dinner that can be served right from the parchment or plated as a meal. I love this method of cooking the halibut as it delivers a juicy and dependable dish every time!

MAKES 1 SERVING

lemon, sliced with some zest plus ends to squeeze the remaining juice directly on the fish

1 (½ lb [227 g]) **halibut fillet**

½ small **shallot**, very thinly sliced

6 whole **cherry tomatoes**, halved

1 clove **fresh garlic**, minced (press directly on flesh of fish)

2 tbsp (30 mL) olive oil

Sea salt and ground pepper to season

freshly chopped parsley for garnish

Preheat oven to 375°F (190°C).

On a cutting board or clean working surface, prepare each pouch by laying the citrus fruit on the bottom and then place the fillet of fish on top of that. Top the fish with the remaining ingredients and slide it into the pouch in that ordered and stacked formation. Drizzle with olive oil and sprinkle with salt and pepper.

Seal the pouch by folding it twice and securing it by laying it the folded side down on a baking sheet so the fish will steam nicely. You can also staple it shut if you wish. Cook these parchment pouches undisturbed for 12 to 15 minutes in the oven. Remove from oven and let sit for 2 to 3 minutes before serving. Garnish with freshly chopped parsley.

+ **SIDE NOTE:** Be careful when opening up the pouch as the steam will be HOT! If you don't want to buy the premade pouches, you can use a large square of parchment paper—place all ingredients in the middle, fold the two long sides together (double fold) and the fold the ends under. It's like wrapping a gift!

+ **NUTRIENT DENSITY FACT:** Halibut in an excellent source of selenium. It is also a very good source of vitamins B_3, B_6 and B_{12} and a good source of phosphorus and vitamin D. There is some choline in there, too.

MEXICAN BEEF BOWL WITH COCAO

A slight hint of chocolate meets heat is the name of this assortment. Grab a bowl or plate, fill it up with this marvelous meat and veggie mixture, dollop with some fresh salsa and dinner is served. The riced cauliflower totally adds a desired consistency that makes the overall composition of this dish something to remember. Pick up some raw organic cocao from your neighborhood health food store today and play around with fun ways to add this rich, antioxidant-packed food into your dishes.

MAKES 2 TO 4 SERVINGS

1½ lbs (681 g) **ground chuck**

2 tbsp (28 g) cooking fat (we use butter/or tallow)

4 **red chili peppers**, finely diced

1 small head of **cauliflower**, grated into a rice-like consistency

2½ tbsp (17 g) **raw cocao powder**

½ cup to 1 cup (120 to 240 mL) **fresh salsa** per serving (page 194)

freshly chopped cilantro and avocado slices and/or Creamy Garlicky Guacomole (page 197) for garnish

In a large cast-iron skillet, begin by cooking the ground meat over medium to high heat until browned. Once cooked through, set aside in a large glass bowl. Keep the leftover juices from the meat in the pan and add the additional cooking fat for the remaining ingredients.

When cooking fat has melted, add in red chili peppers and cook and stir for 5 minutes until softened. Then, add in the grated cauliflower and cook covered for 10 to 15 minutes until it is done to your liking. Use a spoon or fork to mix during this process.

Add the ground meat back into the skillet (with all the juices) and stir together making sure everything is mixed together really well. Continue stirring, while adding in the raw cocao powder. Start with 1 tablespoon (7 g) and mix it together and then taste test to see if you need to add in another tablespoon depending on your preference. Once mixed thoroughly, let simmer over low to medium heat for 10 to 15 minutes. Scoop out portions into bowls and pair with a large dollop of fresh salsa. Garnish with freshly chopped cilantro and slices of avocado or guacamole.

+ **SIDE NOTE:**
  + Feel free to add in additional vegetables if you wish. For efficiency, use a large food processor to grate the cauliflower into a rice-like consistency.
  + If mixture needs a little more moisture add in a splash of water or more cooking fat/oil. Again, start slowly by adding a bit of cocao and stir it in and add more if you wish.

+ **NUTRIENT DENSITY FACT:** Although typically consumed in smaller quantities, cocao has over 4x the RDA for copper. It is also an excellent source of magnesium, manganese and phosphorus as well as a very source of zinc and a good source of potassium and selenium.

ELVIS BURGER

Elvis sure had good taste. At first glance, this combination may seem somewhat odd or irregular, but one never really knows until they try. You MUST try! Originally inspired by a rendition of the Elvis burger on the menu at a greasy spoon here in Toronto, I decided to set out and craft something even more nutritious and delicious that would leave you saying, "Thank you, thank you very much!"

MAKES 4 SERVINGS

12 slices **bacon** (3 slices per serving)

1½ to 2 lbs (681 to 908 g) **ground beef**

1 **egg**, whisked

1 tsp sea salt

1 tsp ground pepper

2 tbsp (28 g) coconut oil

1 large **plantain**, cut into ½" (1.3 cm) angled slices

⅓ cup (67 g) of **sunflower butter** (we recommend SunButter)

large lettuce or Swiss chard leaves and sliced dill pickles for garnish

In a large cast-iron skillet, begin cooking the slices of bacon over medium heat for 15 minutes or until they are cooked to your liking. Remove from skillet and set aside on a plate.

In the meantime in a large glass bowl, combine beef, egg, salt and pepper. Using your hands, get in there to mix and combine really well. Take some of the beef and shape it into a large ball. Continue by pressing it flat into a patty. You will be creating 4 equally sized patties that will be fairly large in size.

Using the same cast-iron skillet, cook the beef patties over medium to high heat for 7 to 10 minutes per side. When the beef patties have had a chance to cook through on one side and you have flipped them over, you will begin frying your plantains in another skillet.

To do this, melt coconut oil over medium to high heat and cook the plantains for 5 minutes on each side or until they become slightly browned and start to caramelize. Turn them using tongs.

Now it's time to build your burger! Begin by stacking the beef patty on the bottom, smear with sunflower butter, add the fried plantains and finally top it all off with the bacon. Serve on lettuce leaves and garnish with a dill pickle on the side.

If you tolerate dairy, add some melted sharp cheddar to your burger.

+ **SIDE NOTE:** Your goal is to try to time everything accordingly in this dish so that it can be served hot! SunButter works best here because it tastes similar to peanut butter, but feel free to play around with different types of nut butters depending on preference, or availability.

+ **NUTRIENT DENSITY FACT:** Sunflower seeds are an excellent source of copper, magnesium, manganese, phosphorus, selenium and vitamin E. They are also a very good source of iron and vitamin B_9 and a good source of zinc and vitamins B_3 and B_6.

SPICY STUFFED ROASTED BELL PEPPERS

A clever friend once told me that the key to making these roasted bell peppers softened to that ideal point is tossing them in the oven for a few minutes on their own before stuffing them with the mixings. I used ground pork as the foundation, but feel free to incorporate your favored choice of ground meat. This is a very compliant meal that you can make ahead of time and then serve later. Any type of bell pepper works here. Have fun playing around with this one!

MAKES 4 SERVINGS

4 medium **bell peppers**, gutted and tops removed

2 tbsp (30 mL) olive oil

1 lb (454 g) **ground pork**

½ tsp sea salt

½ tsp ground pepper

¼ cup (57 g) cooking fat (we used butter/ghee)

1 small head **cauliflower**, grated into a rice-like consistency

6 tbsp (48 g) **capers**, rinsed and drained

3 cups (710 mL) **spicy tomato sauce**, divided (store-bought)

Preheat oven to 375°F (190°C).

Using a small sharp knife, slice off the top of the pepper to create a lid and remove all the seeds and ribbing. Take a silicone brush and coat the peppers with olive oil on all sides, even on the inside.

Place the peppers and the tops in a medium, oven-safe casserole dish. Bake for 30 to 35 minutes or until softened to the touch (use tongs to check, not your fingers). Set aside.

In the meantime on the stovetop, cook the ground pork in a large cast-iron skillet over medium heat. Add salt and pepper and continue stirring occasionally. Cook for about 10 minutes or until browned. When done, reduce heat to low in order to keep warm.

At the same time that the pork is cooking, in a separate skillet, melt butter or ghee over medium heat on the stovetop. Pour in grated cauliflower and stir well. Cook covered for about 10 minutes until cooked to your liking. When done, add the cooked cauliflower to the pork skillet and combine. Stir in the capers and continue to mix thoroughly. At this time, add in half of the amount of tomato sauce, stirring together to create a juicy mixture. When done, top with pepper top.

Once heated, scoop the meat mixture into the cavity of the bell peppers. Top with the remaining amount of tomato sauce and place back into the oven and broil for 5 to 10 minutes. When done, top with pepper top.

If you tolerate dairy, top with your favorite cheese.

+ **NUTRIENT DENSITY FACT:** Capers are a good source of copper, with some iron, vitamin B_2 and vitamin K, as well.

BAKED SAGE AND PROSCIUTTO VEAL MEATBALLS

This dish is a very versatile number. Larger than usual, these meatballs can be gobbled up on their own or added on top of a noodle type dish of your choice. They can be served bare or can be fully clothed with your favorite tomato or dipping sauce. The sage, prosciutto and pork render dollops that are especially saturated in salty wholesome goodness.

MAKES 2 TO 3 SERVINGS

1 tbsp cooking fat, to coat the baking pan

1 lb (454 g) **ground veal**

1 large **egg**, whisked

12 slices **prosciutto**, cut into small pieces

2 tbsp (5 g) chopped **fresh sage**

½ tsp sea salt

½ tsp ground pepper

1½ cups (355 mL) **tomato sauce**, any variety (we used garlic infused)

freshly chopped basil and a squeeze of fresh lemon juice for garnish

Preheat oven to 400°F (204°C).

Prepare a deep metal baking pan or casserole dish by coating the bottom of it with cooking fat. Do so using a silicone brush or a small piece of parchment paper. This will help keep the meatballs from sticking.

Meanwhile, in a large glass bowl, combine veal, egg, prosciutto, sage, salt and pepper. Use your hands to get in there and mix these ingredients together until thoroughly combined. Again, using your hands, form together ping-pong-ball sized meatballs. Once formed, place them in your baking pan. Bake for 25 to 30 minutes, turning once halfway through the cooking time using tongs.

Once cooked, you may eat them just like they are or cover them with tomato sauce. If you want them saucy, turn your oven to broil and heat sauce by cooking everything together for another 5 minutes. Keep a close eye on this dish, as cooking times may vary! Garnish with basil and lemon, if you wish.

If you tolerate dairy, sprinkle in some Parmesan or Gruyere cheese.

+ **SIDE NOTE:** I like to devour these on their own, but you could easily serve them over spaghetti squash, zucchini or sweet potato noodles, too! Great for dipping!

+ **NUTRIENT DENSITY FACT:** Ground veal is a very good source of vitamins B_3 and B_{12}. It is also a good source of phosphorus, selenium, zinc and vitamin B_6. There is also some choline in there, too!

ORANGE-INFUSED KALE SALAD WITH CAULIFLOWER "COUSCOUS"

Inspired by a similar salad sold at the local butcher shop, I opted to make it my own by replacing the couscous with cauliflower rice and changing the complementary secondary ingredients. A raw and natural flair accompanies these greens and molds the kale into a bouquet of sweetness that will nourish your body and make your taste buds sing! Feel free to toss in some leftover roasted meat if you so desire.

MAKES 4 SERVINGS

½ small head of **cauliflower**, grated into a rice-like consistency

2 tbsp (28 g) cooking fat (we used ghee)

½ tsp sea salt

½ tsp ground pepper

1 bunch **leafy kale,** remove from stem and chopped into 1" (2.5 cm) pieces

3 large **carrots,** julienned

½ cup (83 g) **dried figs,** sliced

¾ cup (87 g) **walnuts,** chopped

Orange Citrus Dressing (page 198)

Begin by taking your cauliflower florets and placing them in a large food processor. Pulse on a low setting until the cauliflower becomes grated into a rice-like consistency. In the meantime, melt ghee in a large cast-iron skillet over medium to high heat.

Transfer cauliflower to skillet and season with salt and pepper. Cook covered over medium heat, stirring occasionally for about 10 to 15 minutes or until softened to your liking. Set aside to cool while preparing the rest of the salad.

In a large glass bowl, combine kale, carrots, dried figs and walnuts. Add back in the cooked cauliflower. Pour the orange citrus dressing over top of your salad. Using tongs or your hands, mix thoroughly until coated well.

+ **SIDE NOTE:** To julienne your carrots, you can use a mandolin slicer with a julienne blade or a hand-held peeler works here, too!

+ **NUTRIENT DENSITY FACTS:**
  + Walnuts are an excellent source of copper and manganese, with both over 1x the RDA. They are also a very good source of magnesium, phosphorus and a good source of iron, selenium, zinc and vitamins B_5 and B_6.
  + Dried figs are a good source of copper and iron.

TRADITIONAL NEWFOUNDLAND JIGGS DINNER

We are from Canada, eh! (aka-The Great White North) Ever since my father-in-law Joe was a little boy, he's had fond memories of eating this classic, comforting Sunday meal. A time-honored dish that originated on the East Coast shores of our country, this one-pot dinner yields flaky meat and heavenly vegetables. When you visit your local butcher, be sure to ask for cured brisket and double check that they have it in stock, as sometimes you may need to put in an order ahead of time. A cheesecloth bag is a neat and tidy way to keep your spices simmering away in one place.

MAKES 4 TO 6 SERVINGS

1 large head **green cabbage**, divided and cut into eigths

5 large **carrots**, peeled and cut into 1″ (2.5 cm) chunks

1 large **yellow onion**, cut into large pieces

2 lbs (908 g) **cured brisket** (corned beef)

9 cups water (2 L)

⅓ cup (80 mL) apple cider vinegar

1 (4 oz [115 g]) package **pickling spice blend**

mustard and/or mustard pickles for garnish

Place all ingredients in a large metal stock pot. Then add in water, apple cider vinegar and spices. During this step, make sure to wrap your pickling spice blend in cheesecloth for the duration of the cooking process, so they all stay together! Cover with lid and bring to a boil.

Reduce and simmer at low-medium heat and let cook slowly for 5 hours. Resist the urge to lift the lid, as this will add to the cooking time! When finished, remove spices from the cheesecloth bag and discard.

Use tongs to remove the meat from the Dutch oven first and cut into slices on a cutting board. If you wish, continue by flaking the meat to your desired consistency using a large fork. Plate meat and top with cabbage, carrots, and onions with a slotted spoon in order to remove some of the liquid. Top with your favorite mustard or serve with a side of mustard pickles.

+ **SIDE NOTE:** If you are having difficulty finding the pickling spice blend at a store near you, feel free to create your own by combining coriander, mustard seed, bay leaves, dill seed, cinnamon, ginger, allspice, cayenne, cloves and pepper.

+ **NUTRIENT DENSITY FACT:** Brisket is an excellent source of zinc and vitamin B_{12}. It is also a very good source of selenium and a good source of iron, phosphorus and vitamin B_6. There is some choline in there, too.

POACHED SQUID SALAD

A true winner that is ready in two shakes of a monkey's tail! I like to shop at this local fish market in our neighborhood and every time I go there, I spy this superb-looking squid lying beautifully on the ice. The day I decided to pick it up, I was motivated by a colorful seafood salad that was sitting in the adjacent cooler. The owner encouraged me to poach the squid and assured me it would only take seconds. Right he was! It's an exquisite dish that ends up looking like you spent much longer preparing its delivery. Paired with spicy arugula and sesame dressing, this dish creates an explosion of flavors that pack a punch!

MAKES 2 SERVINGS

4 cups (80 g) **arugula**

2 large **roasted red peppers**, sliced

2 large **carrots**, julienned

2 stalks **celery**, sliced lengthwise

4 cups (1 L) water

1 lb (454 g) **squid**, cut into rings

freshly chopped basil and sesame seeds for garnish

Sesame Ginger Dressing (page 201)

In a large bowl combine arugula, roasted red peppers, carrots and celery. Pour in the dressing, and set aside. In the meantime, fill a medium sized saucepan with water ¾ of the way full. Bring to a boil over high heat on the stovetop. Once you have reached a boil, add in the squid rings and poach for 30 seconds. Remove immediately and stop the cooking process by placing them in an ice bath to cool. Add squid to the large bowl and use tongs to combine everything together. Garnish with freshly chopped basil and sesame seeds. Serve with Sesame Ginger Dressing.

+ NUTRIENT DENSITY FACTS:

+ Squid is an excellent source of selenium and copper (over 2x the RDA). It is also a very good source of vitamin B_{12} and a good source of phosphorus and vitamin B_2.

+ Arugula is an excellent source of vitamin K.

ROASTED TURKEY BREAST WITH APPLE-ORANGE-CRANBERRY SAUCE

At times other than a holiday I get a hankering for turkey, but don't necessarily feel like cooking up an entire bird. Been there, right?! Well, if that is the case, the option of roasting up a couple turkey breasts couldn't be any more fitting. Make sure to buy them from your butcher with the skin on, as this sheath becomes golden and crispy by laying the cooking fat on top as well as underneath the surface of the skin. Cover with a ladle of fruity sauce and enjoy all that this dish has to offer.

MAKES 4 TO 6 SERVINGS

2 (1¾ lb [795 g]) **turkey breasts**, skin on and boneless

5 tbsp (70 g) softened butter, divided

sea salt and ground pepper to season turkey

1 (3 cups [340 g]) package **fresh cranberries**

2 **navel oranges,** segmented

2 **royal gala apples**, peeled and cored

2 tsp (10 mL) **vanilla extract** (good quality)

½ tsp ground cinnamon

Preheat oven to 350°F (176°C).

Rinse turkey breast and pat dry using a paper towel. Take 4 tablespoons (57 g) of softened butter and rub underneath the skin of the turkey. Reserve the remaining butter for the searing process. During this time, don't be afraid to use your hands to create a pocket between the skin and the poultry meat. Next, season generously on both sides of the turkey with salt and pepper.

Heat the remaining butter in a large skillet over high heat on the stovetop. Sear each turkey breast separately, skin side down for 5 minutes or until browned. Once this is done, remove and place on wire-racked baking pan

Roast turkey for 15 to 20 minutes per pound, or until internal temperature reaches 160°F (71°C). Remove turkey and let rest for 15 minutes before slicing.

In the meantime, you can prepare the sauce on the stovetop. In a large food processor combine cranberries, orange segments and apples. Pulse on a medium setting until all these ingredients are blended together to form a chunky consistency. You don't want to blend it for too long, as sauce will continue to reduce and meld together during cooking process.

Transfer this mixture to a medium saucepan. Add in the vanilla and cinnamon and bring to a boil. Reduce and simmer for 20 minutes, stirring occasionally. Slice and plate turkey and top with desired amount of sauce.

+ SIDE NOTE: If you are having difficulty finding fresh cranberries, frozen ones will do the job as well.

CRAB MEAT WITH JUICY MANGO-AVOCADO SALSA

This recipe works well if you are cooking some baked or steamed crab legs or if you have bought a container of lump crabmeat from your local fish/seafood shop that is already prepared and ready to go. Crabmeat has a flaky texture that is slightly sweet in flavor on its own but when coupled with this stimulating and colorful salsa, a whole new element surfaces! This dish is ideal for a light meal that will provide your taste buds with a tropical freshness that will leave you feeling like you are ocean side in the Caribbean. (Wishful thinking right?!)

MAKES 4 SERVINGS

3 **yellow mangos**, cubed into small chunks

1 large **avocado**, cubed into small chunks

3 **mini cucumbers**, cubed into small chunks

4 tbsp (60 mL) olive oil

2 tbsp (30 mL) raspberry balsamic vinegar, divided (regular balsamic is fine too)

2 tbsp (6 g) chopped **fresh chives**

1 lb (454 g) of **crabmeat**, approximately 1 cup (227 g) of meat per person

a squeeze of fresh lemon or lime juice for garnish

In a large glass bowl, combine mango, avocado and cucumber. Add in the olive oil and raspberry balsamic vinegar and top with fresh chives. Using salad tongs, mix gently and combine.

In a separate bowl, add in your crab meat and drizzle with the same respberry balsamic vinegar and olive oil combination. Mix together and coat thoroughly.

Divide up your portions on to plates and top with crabmeat. Garnish with a squeeze of lemon or lime juice.

+ **SIDE NOTE:** You can buy REAL crabmeat at your local fish house. Don't settle for the imitation kind, as this is loaded with lots of nastiness. If buying this prepared, be sure to have a quick look through the crabmeat for any bits of shell that may still be in there!

+ **NUTRIENT DENSITY FACT:** Crab meat is an excellent source of copper and especially vitamin B_{12} (over 4x the RDA). It is also a very good source of selenium and zinc and a good source of phosphorus.

SPICY BRAISED OXTAIL

Oxtail is not actually the tail of an ox, but rather that of beef cattle. I love making this dish in a braised fashion, where the oxtail cooks slow and low in liquid for an extended period of time. If you want to speed up the process, you could also try preparing this meal in a pressure cooker. After a few hours in the Dutch oven, you will lift the lid and be rewarded with fall-off-the-bone meat that is simply delectable and rich with healthful gelatinous properties. The vegetables have a pleasant kick, due to the addition of the scotch bonnets, but also stand up well and yield a smooth texture. Next time you are at the farmers market or butcher shop, have a look around to see if they have any oxtail in stock. You will usually find it sold in packages of 6 or so segments.

MAKES 4+ SERVINGS

---

2 tbsp (28 g) of cooking fat (we used butter)

2 to 2½ lbs (908 g to 1.1 kg) **oxtail**

½ large **rutabaga**, peeled and cut into chunks

5 large **carrots,** peeled and cut into chunks

5 cups (1.1 L) **beef broth and/ or red wine** (combination)

½ tsp sea salt

½ tsp ground pepper

4 dried bay leaves

½ tsp dried thyme

2 to 4 **scotch bonnet peppers**, depending on how spicy you like it

Preheat oven to 350°F (176°C).

In a large cast-iron skillet, heat your cooking fat over medium to high heat on the stovetop. Using tongs, arrange your oxtail in the skillet so that they are not touching one another. Sear on the first side for 5 minutes, undisturbed. Repeat and do the exact same on all of the sides, making sure that all outside edges are browned (total of 20 minutes).

Once seared, remove and place the oxtail in a large, oven-safe Dutch oven. Using the cooking fats and drippings, pour in your chopped rutabaga and quickly brown the outsides for about 5 minutes or so and then add it to the Dutch oven as well. Do the same with the chunks of carrot and then add them to the Dutch oven too.

Pour 1 cup (236 mL) of the beef broth and/or splash of red wine into the cast-iron skillet, to deglaze the pan and remove all the cooked bits and then add this to the Dutch oven. Pour in the rest of your broth (an additional 4 cups [946 mL]) and add your dried spices as well.

On the stovetop, bring to a boil and then cover with lid and place the entire pot into the oven. Braise for an hour and then remove in order to add in your scotch bonnet peppers. Replace the lid and continue cooking in the oven for an additional hour and 45 minutes (cook for 2 to 3 hours total).

Using tongs, remove the scotch bonnet peppers if you wish. Remove meat from each bone by scraping it off with a fork on a cutting board. This will be quite easy to do, as the meat is so tender and succulent. Once this has been done, return all the braised oxtail meat back to the Dutch oven and give it a thorough stir using a large spoon. Season with salt and pepper and serve.

SLOW-COOKER CABBAGE AND BEEF CASSEROLE

Oh, how the home-cooked comforts of my younger days bring back such soothing and delicious memories—like opening the door to the aroma of cabbage rolls! My mother would have spent many hours assembling and cooking this wonderful dish and that is why I have steered clear of this task. All that changed when the idea of layering this delectable meal crossed my mind. How easy is this recipe? Just take all of the ingredients and layer them in the slow cooker and presto! Dinner from the past! When it comes to cooking, one of the things I love is finding new ways to modify familiar family recipes.

MAKES 4+ SERVINGS

2 lbs (908 g) **ground beef**

2 tbsp (28 g) cooking fat

1 **yellow onion**, chopped

3 large **carrots,** shredded

2 tsp (7 g) garlic powder

2 tsp (1½ g) dried basil

2 tsp (2 g) dried thyme

2 tsp (4½ g) paprika

1 tbsp (14 g) coconut oil

1 medium **green cabbage**, cut into 1″ (2.5 cm) strips

1 (3⅓ cups [796 mL]) can of **diced plum tomatoes** and 1 (3⅓ cups [796 mL]) can of **tomato sauce**

In a large cast-iron skillet, cook the ground beef over medium to high heat on the stovetop. When cooked through, set aside in a medium glass bowl. Following this, melt cooking fat in the skillet and start by sautéing the onions first. Cook for 5 minutes and then add in shredded carrot and cook for another 5 minutes. Add the ground beef back in and stir in the garlic powder, dried basil, dried thyme and paprika. Mix thoroughly until mixture is combined.

In the meantime, melt coconut oil in the bottom of the slow cooker. Add in a layer of cabbage, followed by a layer of the beef mixture. Cover the beef with the remaining cabbage and top with the can of diced plum tomatoes and can of tomato sauce. Set slow cooker to high and cook for 4 hours.

COBB SALAD WITH BAY SCALLOPS

Jazz up your traditional Cobb salad with this goody from the sea. In this dish, I put the leftover bacon fat to good use and decided to fry up some bite-sized scallops for something a little bit different! Top that with a drizzle of avocado-lime dressing and you have a meal worthy of some serious merit. The ingredients found within this salad all work in celebration with one another to create a banquet of quality that you will remember. This recipe was created during a phone chit-chat with one of my best friends.

MAKES 4 SERVINGS

1 lb (454 g) **bacon,** crumbled

4 **eggs**, hard boiled and halved

6 small **vine ripe tomatoes** or 3 large, chopped and deseeded

8 cups (450 g) **mixed greens**

2 lbs (908 g) **bay scallops**

Creamy Avocado-Lime Dressing (page 202)

Preheat your oven to 350°F (176°C).

Line a baking sheet with aluminum foil and arrange your slices of bacon on the pan. Bake in the oven for about 20 minutes or until your desired crispiness. Remove the bacon, set aside and crumble using your hands once it has cooled. Pour the leftover bacon fat into a large cast-iron skillet for later.

In the meantime, hard boil your eggs on the stovetop in a small saucepan. Once cooked, pour cold water on top of them and allow them to cool. Also, while this is being done, you can prepare your vegetables so that they are ready to be plated.

Heat the leftover bacon fat in large cast-iron skillet over medium heat on the stovetop. Prepare the bay scallops by making sure they are dry by patting them with a paper towel to remove excess moisture. Pour them into the heated skillet and pan-fry quickly for about 2 to 3 minutes. You do not want to overcook them or they will become tough and rubbery.

Prepare each plate of Cobb salad by dividing all the ingredients equally. Another beautiful way of presenting this dish is to take a medium-sized platter and arrange each ingredient in rows so your guests can serve themselves from there. Drizzle with Creamy Avocado-Lime Dressing and serve.

If you tolerate dairy, add in some blue, asiago or Parmesan cheese.

+ **SIDE NOTES:**
  + When looking for bay scallops, look for the smaller ones. Feeling fancy? Try adding in some shrimp as well.
  + When hardboiling eggs—the rule of thumb we live by is 1 minute per egg and then add an extra minute to the total time on top of that.

NIÇOISE(ISH) SALAD WITH ROASTED FINGERLINGS AND SARDINES

A Niçoise salad is commonly served as an arrangement of green beans, red peppers, anchovies, onions, tomatoes, artichoke hearts, olives, potatoes, hardboiled eggs and tuna. I decided to switch it up a bit here. My version however, is based on the following mishap. In 1978, Julia Child opened a tin of sardines instead of tuna while making a Niçoise Salad. "Forgot to put on my glasses," she said. "Never mind, it just adds a new wrinkle. A wonderful wrinkle indeed. Also, changing things by roasting the potatoes, and red peppers, and topping it all off with an egg that is poached, hardboiled, or softboiled will leave you with a mountain of goodness. A feast for your eyes and your belly.

MAKES 2 SERVINGS

10 **fingerling potatoes**, halved

2 tbsp (28 g) cooking fat (we used duck fat)

1 **red pepper**, sliced and roasted

12 **cherry tomatoes**, halved or quartered

2 (1¼ cup [120 g]) cans of **sardines**, drained and whole

2 **eggs**, poached, hardboiled or softboiled

freshly chopped leaf parsley for garnish

Lemon-Olive Anchovy Dressing (page 201)

Preheat oven to 350°F (176°C).

Place potatoes in a shallow roasting pan or on a baking sheet, along with cooking fat and roast for 30 minutes or until fork tender, stirring occasionally with a large spoon. Add in the bell pepper halfway through cooking time (15 minutes after potatoes go in), as they don't take as long. Toss everything together, making sure all is coated in the duck fat for even roasting.

In the meantime, prepare the rest of your ingredients and make the dressing, so that it is ready to go. When the potatoes and bell peppers are done, pour them into a large bowl and add in the cherry tomatoes. Using tongs, mix everything together.

Plate this salad by scooping out this mixture first and then topping it with sardines. Drizzle it with desired amount of lemon-olive anchovy dressing and top with your egg of choice. Garnish with freshly chopped leaf parsley.

+ **SIDE NOTE:** Want to switch it up? Try topping this salad with your choice of preferred fish. Salmon, tuna or various white fish varieties will work well here.

+ **NUTRIENT DENSITY FACT:** Sardines are an excellent source of vitamin B_{12}, a very good source of phosphorus, selenium, and vitamin B_5 and a good source of copper, iron, sodium, vitamin B_3 and D. There is also some choline in there!

ROASTED BROCCOLI WITH GARLIC AND ANCHOVIES, TOPPED WITH TOASTED ALMONDS

This dish is a far cry from the common thought of broccoli as being boring. Roasting broccoli creates a brilliant color and zest that brings out the full potential that this vegetable has been hiding for oh so long! Turn broccoli haters into broccoli lovers by serving this up as a captivating sidekick that will create an about-face. Steamed broccoli will be sure to remain a distant relative after experimenting with this method that allows for a sweet caramelization to occur.

MAKES 4 SERVINGS

2 heads **broccoli**, cut into florets

3 tbsp (45 mL) cooking fat (we used olive oil)

5 **anchovy fillets**, finely chopped

2 cloves **fresh garlic**, minced

1½ tbsp (22 mL) freshly squeezed **lemon juice**

¼ tsp red pepper flakes

½ tsp sea salt

¼ tsp ground pepper

½ cup (65 g) **sliced almonds**, toasted

Preheat oven to 300°F (148°C).

Pour the broccoli florets into a large glass bowl. In a separate medium glass bowl, combine olive oil, anchovy fillets, garlic, lemon juice, red pepper flakes, salt and pepper and whisk together.

Pour the mixture over top of the broccoli and use tongs to mix, making sure it is coated well. Transfer broccoli to a baking sheet lined with parchment paper or aluminum foil.

Roast in oven for 20 minutes or until slightly browned, turning a couple times throughout this process with a silicone lifter. While the broccoli is roasting, toast almonds in a pan on the stovetop over medium heat for 10 to 15 minutes. Remove broccoli from oven and pour into a large bowl and top with almonds, stirring together gently and serve.

If you tolerate dairy, add in some Parmesan, mozzarella or goat cheese.

+ **SIDE NOTE:** Feel free to broil this dish for the last 3 to 5 minutes to give it that extra crispiness if you wish!

+ **NUTRIENT DENSITY FACT:** Broccoli is an excellent source of vitamin K and a very good source of vitamin C. It is also a good source of vitamin B_9.

GREEN CURRIED BUTTERNUT SQUASH SKILLET

Inspired by Thai cooking flavors, this skillet produces a complete dish that is creamy times a billion. The coconut blend with the green curry paste produces a milky sauce that thickens and becomes even more darling with time. For added effect, we thoroughly enjoy including the sautéed leeks and baby bok choy to round out the disposition of the dish when mated with the butternut squash.

MAKES 4 TO 6 SERVINGS

2 tbsp (28 g) cooking fat (we used coconut oil)

3 **leeks**, chopped into coins

6 **baby bok choy heads**, coarsely chopped

3 tbsp (45 g) **green curry paste**

1 medium **butternut squash**, cubed into ½" (1.3 cm) pieces

1 (14 oz [385 mL]) can full fat **coconut milk**

sea salt and ground pepper to taste

freshly chopped chives or cilantro for garnish

In a wok, heat cooking fat over medium heat. Add in the leeks and stir and cook for 5 to 10 minutes until slightly softened. Then add in the baby bok choy and continue to sauté for another 5 minutes or so while stirring in the green curry paste.

Turn up the heat to medium-high and add in the butternut squash. Pour in the coconut milk and bring to a slight boil. Reduce the heat back to medium and cook covered for 35 to 45 minutes, stirring occasionally.

Once cooked to your liking, turn off heat and let sit covered for 5 to 10 minutes before serving. This will allow the sauce to continue to thicken and become even more flavorful. If you need to add more green curry paste, do so at this time. Sprinkle with salt and pepper. Garnish with freshly chopped chives or cilantro.

+ SIDE NOTE: When looking for a green curry paste, search for one with quality, clean ingredients. Ours included: spices, garlic, lemongrass, galangal, salt, shallot, kefir lime and coriander root. Oh yeah...it may seem like a lot of baby bok choy but, trust me, once cooked it really shrinks down big time!

LOBSTER BISQUE

We are huge seafood people, particularly over the last few years as we have opened up our minds to trying a plethora of new foods from the ocean. I remember feeling so grown up when we cooked a lobster at home for the first time. If you are craving lobster, but don't necessarily want to go through the process of removing the meat, this recipe will still give you that flavor and texture because it works well with already prepared lobster meat. You can find this at your local fish market in a can, usually in the frozen section. If you want to remain more authentic and traditional, feel free to boil your own and create this hearty soup in that way as well.

MAKES 4 SERVINGS

2 tbsp (28 g) cooking fat (we used butter)

4 **pearl onions,** sliced

1 (1¾ cups [400 mL]) can of **coconut cream**

2 cup (470 mL) **broth** (we used vegetable stock)

1 (¾ cup [156 mL]) can **tomato paste**

1 (2¼ cups [320 g]) can prepared **lobster meat,** divided

1 tbsp (6 g) red curry powder

2 tsp (4) cayenne

sea salt and ground pepper to taste

freshly chopped chives and avocado slices for garnish

In a large Dutch oven, heat the cooking fat. Start by sautéing your pearl onions until softened. Add in the coconut cream, broth, tomato paste and half of the amount of lobster meat. Cook and stir for 15 minutes over medium heat. Using an immersion hand blender, puree the soup to your desired consistency.

Add in the remaining amount of lobster meat (keeping it in chunks) and bring to a slow boil. Reduce the heat and stir in your spices. Continue to cook on the stovetop for an additional 20 to 30 minutes. Ladle into soup bowls. Garnish with freshly chopped chives and avocado slices.

+ **SIDE NOTE:** If you are sensitive to spice, try using half the amounts, or add them in slowly and taste test along the way.

MOROCCAN LAMB BURGERS

When you think of burgers, beef burgers usually come to mind. Try switching it up some with this luscious patty that is inspired by Moroccan cuisine. The base of cumin-fried onions and the light topping of lemon cucumber bring balance and harmony to this dish. Plan ahead by picking up some harissa sauce from a Middle Eastern food shop in your area or online if that is more accessible for you! You won't want to leave that ingredient out. That is truly what brings these burgers to life and gives them some fire!

MAKES 4 TO 6 SERVINGS

FOR THE LAMB PATTY

2 lbs (908 g) **ground lamb**

2 tbsp (30 g) **harissa sauce**, store bought

handful **fresh parsley,** chopped

½ tsp cinnamon

1 tsp paprika

½ tsp coriander

1 tsp sea salt

½ tsp ground pepper

FOR THE BASE AND THE TOPPING

2 medium **yellow onions,** thinly sliced

1 tsp ground cumin

½ large **English cucumber,** spiraled with sea salt, ground pepper and olive oil

a squeeze of fresh lemon for garnish

In a large glass bowl, combine the ground lamb, harissa sauce, fresh parsley, spices, salt and pepper. Using your hands, get in there and mix together thoroughly.

Next, roll the lamb mixture into a medium-sized ball and press into ½ inch (1.3 cm) thick patties. In a large cast-iron skillet on the stove or on the grill on the barbeque, cook for 4 to 5 minutes a side, turning with a lifter.

Meanwhile, sauté the onion in a separate skillet over medium to high for 10 to 15 minutes. Stir regularly. In the last 5 minutes, add in the ground cumin while continuing to stir. At the same time, prepare spiraled or julienned cucumber and season with salt and pepper. Plate this dish by building the burger with a foundation of sautéed onions first, then the patty and finally top with cucumber spirals. Garnish with a squeeze of fresh lemon juice.

+ **SIDE NOTE:** Feel free to serve on lettuce leaves as well. As leftovers, these burgers remained super juicy and delicious—even the next day! You can find harissa sauce at many specialty/Middle Eastern ethnic food shops and on various online stores as well. Highly recommended, as it is essential to making these burgers extra flavorful, spicy and moist! Harissa sauce is usually made of hot peppers, garlic, coriander, caraway and salt. It's commonly found in a small jar or can.

+ **NUTRIENT DENSITY FACT:** Ground lamb is an excellent source of Vitamin B_{12}. It is also a very good source of zinc and selenium. It is a good source of ion, phosphorus, vitamin B_3 and has some choline.

TWICE-BAKED STUFFED SWEET POTATO

Back in the day, I used to always enjoy twice-baked stuffed potatoes at my friend's house over the Christmas holidays. She would whip these up by loading them with tons of amazing ingredients. I remember looking forward to them every single time we went to visit at that time of the year. A few Christmases ago I wasn't able to make it there to see them, so I decided to come up with a rendition of my own. The end result is nothing short of golden, as these sweet potato skins are literally overflowing with a mound of "oh my gosh!"

MAKES 2 TO 4 SERVINGS

½ lb (227 g) **bacon**, crumbled into pieces

2 large **sweet potatoes**, halved

1 lb (454 g) **ground turkey**

1 small **red onion**, finely diced

4 cloves of **fresh garlic**, minced

2 tbsp (13 g) smoked chipotle powder

1 tsp ground cinnamon

1 tsp ground nutmeg

sea salt and ground pepper, to taste

freshly chopped chives, dried cranberries and a pat of butter for garnish

Preheat oven to 350°F (176°C).

Line a baking sheet with aluminum foil and lay out your slices of bacon. Bake them in the oven for 20 minutes or until you have reached your desired crispiness. Remove and set aside to cool. Carefully drain the excess bacon fat into a small jar for later.

Next, slice the sweet potatoes evenly in half. Take some of the leftover bacon fat and brush on the flesh side of the sweet potato using a silicone brush. Place the halves face down on the baking pan. Turn the temperature up to 375°F (190°C) for 35 to 45 minutes or until the inside is tender (time may vary depending on size of sweet potato—you can check for doneness by using a fork to gently press on the skin side). When they are done, set aside and allow time to cool for 10 minutes.

In the meantime, in a large cast-iron skillet, brown the ground turkey over medium to high heat. Remove and set aside in a medium glass bowl. In the same skillet, add in some of the reserved bacon fat and heat it up on the stovetop. Add in onion, and cook and stir for 10 minutes or until softened. Next, add in the garlic and continue cooking for another 5 minutes. Re-add the ground turkey and mix everything together.

Once mixed, take the meat mixture and pour it into a large glass bowl. Carefully scoop out the insides of the baked sweet potatoes and add it into the same bowl, combining thoroughly as you spice it up with the chipotle powder, cinnamon and nutmeg. Next, take the empty skins and fill them up with the mixture from the bowl. Place stuffed skins back on the pan and broil for 5 minutes or so until they are slightly browned and crispy on top. (Keep a close eye on them, as you don't want them to burn!)

Remove from oven and sprinkle with salt and pepper. Garnish with freshly chopped chives, dried cranberries and top with a pat of butter.

If you can tolerate dairy, add in and sprinkle with your favorite kind of cheese.

SANTA FE OMELET WITH SLICED AVOCADO

This omelet is perfect for a weekend meal when you may have a little more time to devote to the kitchen. It requires a wee bit more preparation and patience, as the tomato concasse is at its best when it's given time to intermingle and associate with the other ingredients. When the tomatoes are cooked in this manner, they form a filling and topping that is just a teensy bit more special than your regular omelet. An impeccable folded omelet can be achieved through the method described below—a foolproof technique we learned many years ago at a breakfast joint in our neighborhood.

MAKES 2 SERVINGS

4 **vine ripe tomatoes,** skinned, seeded and diced

water to fill ½ saucepan

2 tbsp (28 g) cooking fat (we used ghee)

1 medium **yellow onion,** thinly sliced

3 small **bell peppers** (red, green and yellow—one of each), julienne sliced

2 tsp (5 g) Cajun spice blend (salt, garlic, paprika, onion)

¼ tsp dried chili flakes

¼ tsp ground pepper

¼ cup (60 mL) water

6 **eggs,** whisked

2 **avocados,** sliced

Take the tomatoes and remove the core with a small sharp knife or an apple corer. Turn it over and gently score the skin on the bottom with an x. In a saucepan, over high heat, bring water to a boil. Once boiling, place tomatoes in water for 25 seconds. Remove them using a slotted spoon and place them in a medium glass bowl filled with ice water (this will stop the cooking process and help with the skin-removal of the tomatoes). Take them out and place on a cutting board. Peel off the skins and seed the tomato so that you are just left with the outer part. Dice that up and set aside in a small glass bowl.

Meanwhile, in a large cast-iron skillet, melt cooking fat over medium to high heat. Add in the onion and cook and stir for about 10 minutes until translucent. Following this, add in the bell peppers and sauté for 20 minutes (practice patience here, as you want them to slowly cook down and become softened).

Add in the spices and water, along with the tomatoes. Continue to let sweat and simmer over low to medium heat for 5 minutes. In a medium glass bowl, crack eggs and whisk together. In a separate non-stick skillet, gently pour in half of your egg mixture and start to cook omelet on low to medium heat for about 5 minutes. In the meantime, turn your oven setting to broil. Next, add in ¼ of your tomato concasse mixture for the inside of your omelet. To finish off the dish, put oven-safe skillet under the broiler for 3 to 5 minutes. Remove and have a plate ready on the counter. Slowly tilt your skillet and allow the omelet to slide out onto the plate, until it reaches halfway. Once it does, a quick flick of the wrist and the other half will cover the mix and create a perfect fold. Top with a couple spoonfuls of tomato concasse mixture and avocado. Repeat these instructions for remaining omelet.

LAMB TAGINE

Sitting in a yurt over a lovely dinner here in Toronto, two of my good friends were raving to my husband and me about many of the delicious recipes they have created using their tagine pot. After this conversation, they lent us theirs so that we could check it out for ourselves. Let's just say we quickly fell in love. So much so that we went to the little shop where they bought theirs and decided to purchase one of our own. In case you aren't familiar with it, a tagine pot is a clay cooking device that has a solid base and a cone-shaped lid. Its unique design works so that the moisture is constantly being recycled back into the cooking of the food. Typical in Moroccan cooking, this method promotes a huge return on investment. Little effort is needed and it lends you a dish that is infused with spice and the bonus of presenting it from stovetop to table, right in the foundation of the pot.

MAKES 2 SERVINGS

10 **dried apricots,** soaked and sliced

1 tbsp (14 g) ghee

1 to 1½ lbs (454 g to 681 g) **boneless leg of lamb**

1 small **red onion,** diced

1 tsp garlic powder

1½ tbsp (12 g) **ras el hanout**

½ tsp ground ginger

¼ tsp ground cinnamon

2 tbsp (30 mL) to ¼ cup (60 mL) water, depending on the size of the tagine base

1 medium **vine ripe tomato,** coarsely chopped

chopped parsley and crushed pistachios for garnish

Place the dried apricots in a small bowl and cover with water to soak.

In the bottom of your tagine, melt cooking fat and brown the lamb on the stovetop over medium to high heat. During this time, use tongs to turn the pieces over and sear for 10 minutes total. When browned, scoop out with a slotted spoon and set aside.

Next, add in the onion and sauté for 5 minutes. Add in the garlic and cook and stir for another 2 minutes. Then, add in the spices and mix together with water. Let simmer for a couple minutes. Re-add the lamb. Top that with the chopped tomato and place the lid on the tagine. Let simmer on the stovetop for 45 minutes, over medium heat.

When you have reached this time, remove the lid and add in the apricots. Place the lid back on and cook for another 10 to 15 minutes. Remove the lid and let sit for about 10 minutes. Season with salt and pepper. Garnish with freshly chopped parsley and crushed pistachios.

+ SIDE NOTE: If the pot begins to overflow during the cooking process, quickly lift the lid, and then you will be back in business. Feeling extra fancy? Toss in some preserved lemons for an added tweak with a zing.

ESPRESSO AND CACAO RUBBED ROAST BEEF AU JUS

What's not to love in this one? Beef, wine, chocolate, coffee—a total dream, right? Well pretty much, other than missing chips and fries! Gosh...I love chips and fries! Anyways, back to the beef. This version is such a welcome rendition for your regular roast beef dinner. The dark rub creates a rich crust that is pleasantly bitter and full of life when paired with the sweetness of the jus. Turn leftovers (if you have any), into a wonderful salad that focuses on fresh antipasto ingredients (see page 97 for Shaved Roast Beef Salad). Spruce up Sunday night dinner with this tender roast, which is a little bit different than your everyday roast.

SERVES 4 TO 6

2½ lbs (1.1 kg) **sirloin tip roast**

¾ cup (180 mL) **Madeira wine**, divided

3 tbsp (18 g) **raw cacao powder**

2 tbsp (12 g) finely **ground espresso**

1 tsp chipotle powder

½ tsp sea salt

1 cup (240 mL) **beef broth**

1 tsp garlic powder

1 tsp onion powder

salt and pepper to taste

Place the roast in a large re-sealable bag or casserole dish and pour in ¼ cup (60 mL) Madeira wine. Let marinate in the liquid for at least 1 hour. Before you cook the meat, let the roast come to room temperature on the counter.

Preheat oven to 450°F (232°C).

In a small glass bowl, combine raw cacao, ground espresso, chipotle powder and salt. Remove the roast from the marinade and place on a cutting board. Sprinkle the rub on all sides of the roast, making sure to press it into the meat with your hands, so that it is coated entirely.

Place the roast on a wire-racked baking pan. Roast in the oven at 450°F (232°C) for the first 20 minutes. This will help create a nice crust on the outside of the meat. Reduce the oven temperature to 300°F (148°C) and roast for an additional 55 minutes or until the meat reaches an internal temperature of 130°F (54°C) for medium-rare.

Once you have checked it with the meat thermometer, remove roast from the pan and let sit on a clean cutting board for 5 to 10 minutes covered with aluminum foil before slicing. In the meantime, using any leftover ingredients plus some additional flavorings, you will create the jus in the baking pan. Remove wire rack and place the same pan on the stovetop. Begin pouring in the beef broth and ½ cup (120 mL) Madeira wine and bring to a boil, stirring continuously. While stirring, add in the garlic powder, onion powder, salt and pepper.

Slice roast across the grain and plate. Enjoy with a drizzle of jus on top, alongside your favorite side dish.

REALLY RED WALDORF SALAD

This really red salad is a ravishing twist on your traditional Waldorf. My signature item that makes it so unique is the awesome addition of beets to the mix. Their natural ruby coloring and earthy undertones, combined with the dressing, render a final product that is oh so vibrant and lively when placed in endive or lettuce leaves. Can be enjoyed as a slightly warm dish or as a cold meal after being placed in the refrigerator for a period of time. It's a creamy chicken salad at its finest.

MAKES 2 TO 3 SERVINGS

3 large purple/red **beets**, cubed

2 (½ lb [227 g]) **chicken breasts**, cubed (or thighs)

½ cup (59 g) **raw walnuts**, chopped

20 **red grapes**, halved

1 **apple,** peeled and chopped (we used Fuji)

Creamy Coconut-Mustard Dressing (page 205)

Preheat oven to 375°F (190°C).

Wrap the beets separately in aluminum foil and place on a small baking sheet. Place chicken breasts in a medium-sized casserole dish and bake all together for 35 minutes. Remove the chicken and continue cooking the beets for an additional 10 minutes.

Once you remove them from the oven, let cool. Peel and cube beets and cube chicken. Combine chicken, beets, walnuts, grapes and apple in a large glass bowl. Drizzle with Creamy Coconut-Mustard Dressing and mix together using tongs to make sure everything is coated. The beets will turn everything a reddish color. This is supposed to happen. Eat immediately or let cool in fridge and then eat later.

If you can tolerate dairy, add in goat, Parmesan or Roquefort cheese.

EGGS BENEDICT WITH POTATO LATKES

A wonderful stackable meal that is just simply ambrosial. The thick and creamy hollandaise sauce is a wondrous addition that lusciously flows over top of the rest of the dish. Want more? Well, under that you have the rich gooey yolks that are an excellent source of choline. Keep cutting in, and you will reach even more excellence with some classic Canadian bacon and a solid bottom infrastructure of crispy potato latkes. You can use white potatoes, yams or sweet potatoes here...the choice is yours!

MAKES 4 SERVINGS (BASED ON 2 EGGS PER PERSON)

FOR THE BACON

1 tbsp (14 g) cooking fat (we used lard)

8 slices **Canadian bacon**

FOR THE EGGS

8 chicken **eggs,** or 4 duck eggs, poached

6 cups (1.4 L) of water

1 tbsp (15 mL) of apple cider vinegar

FOR THE POTATO LATKES

2 tbsp (28 g) cooking fat (we used duck fat)

2 large **Yukon Gold potatoes**, peeled and finely grated

½ medium **yellow onion**, finely grated

1 **egg**, whisked

¼ tsp sea salt

¼ tsp ground pepper

FOR THE HOLLANDAISE SAUCE (ALSO, SEE PAGE 207)

3 **egg yolks**

1 tbsp (15 mL) freshly squeezed **lemon juice**

1 tbsp (15 mL) warm water

¼ tsp sea salt

½ cup (120 mL) melted ghee (allow time to cool, as you do not want it warm/hot)

¼ tsp cayenne pepper

1 tsp hot sauce (optional but if you do we recommend Sriracha)

finely chopped parsley for garnish

Preheat oven 225°F (107°C).

In a large cast-iron skillet, heat cooking fat over medium to high heat on the stovetop. Place the slices of Canadian bacon in the skillet and cook for 5 minutes per side until browned and turn using the tongs. Once cooked, remove and place in a casserole dish and put in the oven to keep warm.

At the same time, take the grated potato and place it in a cheesecloth or tea towel and wring tightly over the sink to remove as much water as possible. Then, take the potato and onion and place in a large glass bowl. Combine with the egg, salt and pepper and mix together thoroughly. Using your hands, press together to make small patties. Ahead of time, heat your cooking fat in a separate cast-iron skillet over medium to high heat on the stovetop. Gently place the potato latkes in the pan and fry for 10 minutes or so each side, turning over every 2 minutes. Cook until crispy and golden brown. When done, place in the casserole dish to keep warm with the bacon.

Next, prepare the Hollandaise sauce that will be the topping for this dish. In a medium measuring cup, add in the egg yolks, lemon juice, warm water and sea salt. Take your immersion blender and lower it into the measuring cup. Turn it on and blend for a few seconds and then begin slowly pouring in the melted room temperature ghee in a light, steady stream. Once blended to your liking, remove the immersion blender and add in the spice and/or hot sauce, stirring thoroughly. Transfer to a small saucepan and keep warm on the stovetop over low heat.

Lastly, to poach the eggs, put the water in a saucepan, bring it to a slight boil and add in the apple cider vinegar. Once ready, place each egg in a small coffee mug and gently place the mug into the hot water. Then, gently ease the egg into the water and cook for 5 minutes or until the egg whites have solidified. Use a slotted spoon to remove the eggs. Pat the eggs dry of any excess water with paper towel and set aside. Plate the dish by layering the items: first the latke, then the bacon and egg and finally top the tower with a generous drizzle of the Hollandaise sauce. Salt and pepper and garnish with finely chopped parsley.

+ SIDE NOTE: When grating the Yukon Gold potato and the yellow onion, use a food processor or hand grater on the finest setting. Also, remember to allow the ghee to cool a little bit before pouring it into the measuring cup, as you do not want it to cook the eggs within the Hollandaise sauce.

LEMON CAPER OVEN BAKED TROUT WITH FRESH DILL AND BROWNED BUTTER

Cooking a fish whole like this is just about as straightforward and uncomplicated as it gets. I purchased one large trout from a fish stand at the farmers market, but you could opt for two smaller ones if you wish. Kindly ask them to clean and prepare the fish so that it is all ready to go for you! With that done, all you have to do is create the oil-based rub and you are off to the races. Time it for 20 or so in the oven, and you are left with a reasonably priced main that can feed up to 4 hungry dinner guests. Tie it all together with the light nutty flavor of drizzled browned butter.

MAKES 2 TO 4 SERVINGS

1 (2 lbs [908 g]) **whole trout**, cleaned and gutted

¼ cup (60 mL) olive oil

¼ tsp coarse sea salt

¼ tsp ground pepper

1 tbsp (3 g) **fresh dill,** chopped

2 tbsp (18 g) **capers**, rinsed, drained and chopped

2 cloves **fresh garlic**, minced

additional sea salt and ground pepper to season

¼ cup (56 g) butter

1 **lemon**, ½ sliced into rounds and the other ½ freshly squeezed juice

Preheat oven to 400°F (204°C).

Rinse your fish and pat dry on the inside and outside with paper towel. In a small bowl combine olive oil, salt, pepper, dill, capers, garlic and lemon juice. Using a silicone brush, coat the inside and the outside of the fish generously.

Season the outside skin of the fish with some additional salt and pepper. Stuff the inside of the trout with some slices of lemon.

Place stuffed fish on a baking sheet lined with aluminum foil. Bake it in the oven for 20 minutes or until the meat easily flakes away from the skin (check using a fork). Remove and let rest for 10 minutes before serving.

In the meantime, in a heavy metal saucepan, add in the butter. Heat over medium to high heat bringing it to a slight boil, stirring continuously. Reduce heat to low and continue to stir, using a silicone spoon, until the color of the butter turns a light brown tone, about 5 minutes. Once achieved, this will act as a complementary drizzle that holds a slight hint of nuttiness.

+ **NUTRIENT DENSITY FACT:** Trout is an excellent source of vitamin B_{12}. It is also a good source of copper, magnesium, phosphorus, selenium, vitamins B_1, B_2, B_3 and B_5.

INSIDE-OUT BISON BURGERS

Bison is a very lean cut of meat. I enjoy these burgers the most when cooked to a medium-rare finale. My creation and formulation of the idea behind this inside-out burger is just as the name suggests. What you find in the outside topping is also cleverly combined within the actual patty to give it a double dose of beauty. They work hand-in-hand to enhance the overall character and structure of the burger. As an added perk, enjoy with your favorite mustard!

MAKES 4+ SERVINGS

3 tbsp (43 g) cooking fat (we used butter)

2 medium **yellow onions**, chopped

2 (4 cups [228 g]) packages **mushrooms** of choice, finely chopped (we did a mixture of baby bella and portabella)

4 (¼" [.6 cm] slices) **smoked ham**, cubed into small pieces

2 tsp (5 g) dry mustard powder

½ tsp sea salt

½ tsp ground pepper

2 lbs (908 g) **ground bison**

1 tbsp (15 g) cooking fat (we used lard or tallow)

a generous amount of **fresh horseradish**, grated

sliced tomatoes and greens or lettuce leaves for garnish

In a large cast-iron skillet, melt your cooking fat over medium heat on the stovetop. Add in your onions and cook and stir for 10 minutes until softened. Add in your mushrooms and continue to cook and stir for an additional 15 minutes. Close to the end, add in your smoked ham, dry mustard, salt and pepper and sauté for another 2 minutes. Turn the temperature down to low and let simmer.

In a large glass bowl, combine ground bison with half of your cooked onion-mushroom-ham mixture from the skillet. Using tongs to start (it will still be warm), mix all together. You can also use your hands after a few minutes (once it has cooled) to continue to combine all the ingredients together.

Meanwhile in a separate skillet, melt cooking fat over medium heat. Take the ground bison mixture and use your hands to roll up balls of meat and then flatten them into patties (½ inch [1.3 cm] thick). Cook patties in batches over medium heat for a total of 16 minutes, turning every 4 minutes. These can also be grilled on the barbeque outdoors. Remove burger patties and plate. Top with a spoonful of reserved onion-mushroom-ham mixture and a pinch of fresh horseradish. Enjoy while dipping in your favorite mustard. Garnish with sliced tomatoes and serve on greens or lettuce leaves.

+ NUTRIENT DENSITY FACT: Ground bison is an excellent source of vitamin B_{12} and a very good source of selenium. It is also a good source of iron, phosphorus, zinc and vitamin B_6.

DIPS, DRESSINGS AND DRIZZLES

Making homemade salad dressing seriously couldn't be any easier! Here's all you need to do. Basically, choose an oil, add in some acidic juices, toss in additional ingredients for flavoring or texture—and that's a wrap! For most of my dressings, I just pour everything into a small mason jar, put on the lid and give it a few shakes... and voilà, finished! Aside from that, a small food processor can come in handy, if you are making a dressing where you want everything whipped up super smooth. When making your own mayonnaise, life gets even easier by using a handy dandy immersion hand blender: a tool that will give you results in less than a minute! Have fun playing around with these combinations. Making your own salad dressing will basically guarantee that you will never go back to the commercial, store-bought dressing varieties that are typically filled with nasty oils and lots of junk!

+ HOT 'N' SPICY SALSA

+ CREAMY GARLICKY GUACAMOLE

+ CLASSIC SEXTON BALSAMIC VINAIGRETTE

+ ORANGE CITRUS DRESSING

+ SESAME GINGER DRESSING

+ LEMON-OLIVE ANCHOVY DRESSING

+ SUN-DRIED TOMATO AND BASIL VINAIGRETTE

+ CREAMY AVOCADO-LIME DRESSING

+ HONEY-MUSTARD DRESSING

+ CREAMY COCONUT-MUSTARD DRESSING

+ BALSAMIC REDUCTION

+ MARVELOUS MAYONNAISE

+ SRIRACHA SPIKED HOLLANDAISE SAUCE

HOT 'N' SPICY SALSA

This is a perfect accompaniment to complement all different types of meat, as a topping on your eggs or even a salad dressing (nachos, too). Best enjoyed when tomatoes are in season in your area, as nothing beats the taste of garden-fresh goodness that they provide! This recipe offers an excellent way to use up those tomatoes if they are growing like wildfire in your backyard patch. If you can tolerate corn, splurge for some good quality tortilla chips if you so choose.

MAKES 3 CUPS (700 ML)

6 large **vine ripe tomatoes**, deseeded and diced

½ large **white onion**, finely diced

1 **jalapeño pepper** or 1 **hot pepper**, finely diced

¼ cup (60 mL) freshly squeezed **lime (or lemon)** juice

a handful of **fresh cilantro**, chopped

sea salt and ground pepper to taste

Wash all the veggies thoroughly and chop all ingredients finely (depending on how chunky you want it). Combine and mix well. Add in your lemon or lime juice and freshly chopped cilantro while continuing to mix together. Season with desired amount of salt and pepper. Grab some vegetables to dip or use as a side or a spread/topping on your meat dishes and salads.

+ **SIDE NOTE:** If you don't like things hot 'n' spicy, then you can omit the jalapeño/hot peppers and sub in some fresh garlic or chopped up blueberries. This adds a unique and interesting spin on things! Regardless, this condiment dish is super light and fresh tasting—perfect for barbeque season or a summertime party. Make sure you allow time for a few hours (overnight even better) for this salsa to set in the fridge. This allows all the flavors to meld together.

+ **NUTRIENT DENSITY FACT:** Fresh cilantro is an excellent source of vitamin K (2.5x the RDA) and a good source of copper and vitamins A and C.

CREAMY GARLICKY GUACAMOLE

Birthday parties, staff luncheons, Christmas, Easter, New Year's and well basically any occasion that you name, this tasty condiment meets the mark. I honestly feel like I bring this to just about every single function that we have to go to. It has become that signature dish if you know what I mean. We love to put it on just about everything. I may even be known as someone who eats it right out of the bowl. It's so good that I actually think I should package it up and sell it! HA!

MAKES 4 CUPS (1 L)

4 to 6 large **avocados** (ripe and soft, but not too soft to the touch)

½ pint **grape tomatoes**, finely chopped

5 cloves **fresh garlic**, minced

¼ cup to ⅓ cup (60 to 77 mL) freshly squeezed **lime juice**

handful **fresh cilantro**, chopped (we use lots!)

sea salt and ground pepper to taste

hot sauce or chopped jalapeño peppers for garnish

In a large glass bowl, squash the avocado with a large fork or a potato masher. Do this until most of the large chunks have been smoothed out. Then, add in the tomato, garlic, lime juice, fresh cilantro, salt and pepper and continue stirring together until you have reached your desired consistency.

If you want it to be really creamy, and don't want to do this by hand, feel free to toss everything in a large food processor and blend together that way.

+ **SIDE NOTE:** If you like a little spice in your life and want to kick it up a notch, throw in a few splashes of hot sauce at the end or some chopped jalapeños.

+ **NUTRIENT DENSITY FACT:** Fresh garlic (raw) is an excellent source of vitamin B_6 and a very good source of manganese. It is also a good source of copper, selenium and vitamin C.

CLASSIC SEXTON BALSAMIC VINAIGRETTE

Throw away your a million ingredient commonly store-bought brands and fix up just about any salad with this versatile dressing. This go-to, good ol' faithful concoction is a simple way to dress your greens while feeling good about it!

MAKES APPROXIMATELY ½ CUP (120 ML)

2 tbsp (30 mL) balsamic vinegar

¼ (60 mL) cup olive oil

2 tbsp (30 g) **grainy mustard**

1½ (23 mL) tbsp freshly squeezed **lemon juice**

1 clove **fresh garlic**, minced

sea salt and pepper to taste

Add all ingredients into a small mason jar and shake well to combine.

+ **SIDE NOTE:** Feel free to double or triple all dressing recipes if you need more or wish to store in the fridge.

+ **NUTRIENT DENSITY FACT:** Mustard is good source of selenium.

ORANGE CITRUS DRESSING

To mix things up once in a while, try this citrusy summer dressing as a pleasing alternative to jazz things up. This combination adds a refreshing zing to your vegetables and many fish/seafood dishes while remaining light and sunny.

MAKES APPROXIMATELY ½ CUP (120 ML)

½ cup (120 mL) freshly squeezed **navel orange juice**

3 tbsp (45 mL) freshly squeezed **lemon juice**

¼ cup (60 mL) olive oil

2 tbsp (30 g) **grainy mustard**

1 tbsp (15 mL) red wine vinegar

salt and pepper to taste

Add all ingredients into a small mason jar and shake well to combine.

+ **NUTRIENT DENSITY FACT:** Olive oil is an excellent source of vitamin E and a very good source of vitamin K.

SESAME GINGER DRESSING

This Asian-inspired dressing is a fusion that provides a beautiful balance of sweet and savory. Serve this to your family and friends and they will definitely be asking for this recipe. Simply put, it's a real winner that pairs really well with arugula as the green in your salad.

MAKES APPROXIMATELY ½ CUP (120 ML)

¼ cup (60 mL) olive oil

1 tbsp (15 mL) white wine vinegar

½ tbsp (7.5 mL) **sesame oil**

½ tsp **red curry paste**

2 tbsp (30 mL) **coconut aminos**

½ tsp **fresh ginger**, finely grated

½ tbsp (10 g) **raw honey** (optional)

¼ tsp sea salt

¼ tsp ground pepper

Add all ingredients into a small mason jar and shake well to combine.

LEMON-OLIVE ANCHOVY DRESSING

This dressing really packs a punch of flavor. Don't be shy—go ahead and be a little more adventurous by trying anchovies in your dressing. They are honestly a really nice touch that brings something special to the table.

MAKES APPROXIMATELY ½ CUP (120 ML)

3 **anchovy fillets**, rinsed and minced

8 **Kalamata olives**, finely chopped

10 **capers**, rinsed and minced

1 tbsp (15 g) **grainy mustard**

3 tbsp (45 mL) freshly squeezed **lemon juice**

¼ cup (60 mL) olive oil

½ tsp ground pepper

Add all ingredients into a small mason jar and shake well to combine.

SUN-DRIED TOMATO AND BASIL VINAIGRETTE

This dressing brings me back to my university days. I used to love sun-dried tomato dressing. Remember when it was like the "it" thing!? Say yes, don't make me feel old. Then I feel like I went through a long stretch without it, but now it is back and back in full force! It holds an Italian surge of flavor that will boost any salad into another realm.

MAKES APPROXIMATELY ½ CUP (120 ML)

¼ cup (60 mL) olive oil

1 tbsp (15 mL) balsamic vinegar

2 tbsp (30 mL) water

¼ tsp sea salt

¼ tsp ground pepper

1½ tbsp (16 g) **sun-dried tomatoes**

1 tbsp (11 g) sliced **pimentos**

1 clove **fresh garlic**

4 **fresh basil** leaves

Add everything in a small food processor and pulse until the desired consistency has been reached.

CREAMY AVOCADO-LIME DRESSING

If you love guacamole, you will love this dressing. Even if you don't love guacamole, chances are you will adore this. As the title states, it's thick and substantial and provides a solid means of finishing off any salad. Enjoy this dressing knowing that you are nourishing your body with healthy fats.

MAKES APPROXIMATELY ½ CUP (120 ML)

½ **avocado**

3 tbsp (45 mL) freshly squeezed **lime juice**

1 tbsp (15 mL) **lemon juice**

1 clove **fresh garlic**

a handful of **fresh cilantro**

¼ tsp sea salt

¼ tsp ground pepper

3 tbsp (45 mL) olive oil

2 tbsp (30 mL) water

Add everything in a small food processor and pulse, until the desired consistency has been reached. More water or oil will help you achieve this.

HONEY-MUSTARD DRESSING

Start with a really good quality Dijon mustard. Play around with this one, as many specialty shops and delis offer all different types of mustards to choose from. This dressing isn't overpowering and presents an option that holds a little bit of tartness, but a slight sweetness on the finish.

MAKES APPROXIMATELY ½ CUP (120 ML)

¼ cup (60 mL) olive oil

2 tbsp (30 g) **Dijon mustard**

1 tbsp (20 g) **raw honey** (unpasteurized)

2 tbsp (30 mL) **lemon juice**

1 tbsp (15 mL) **lime juice**

¼ sea salt

¼ tsp ground pepper

Add all ingredients into a small mason jar and shake well to combine.

CREAMY COCONUT-MUSTARD DRESSING

Whip up some of this smooth and satisfying dressing with that little bit of leftover coconut milk that you don't know what to do with, but don't want to throw out! This is a nice simple dressing that can be made with only 3 ingredients if you are in a rush and want something a little different to toss in your lunch bag.

MAKES APPROXIMATELY ½ CUP (120 ML)

3 tbsp (45 g) **Dijon mustard**

¼ cup (60 mL) **coconut milk**

1 tbsp (15 mL) olive oil

2 tbsp (30 mL) **lemon juice**

¼ tsp sea salt

½ tsp ground pepper

Add all ingredients into a small mason jar and shake well to combine.

BALSAMIC REDUCTION

All you need is balsamic vinegar for the reduction. Yes, that is correct—just that! That's it, that's all, my friends. Of course, if you want to infuse it with some fresh herbs then you can do so. Just remember: think about how much balsamic reduction drizzle you want to end up with and double the starting amount to create that. Oh yeah, the better quality the balsamic, the yummier the end product will taste. Trust me on this one!

MAKES ½ CUP (120 ML)

1 cup (240 mL) **balsamic vinegar**

fresh herbs, optional

Pour the balsamic vinegar into a heavy saucepan and bring to a boil over high heat. As soon as your balsamic starts to boil, immediately reduce it to a low to medium temperature and let simmer for 15 minutes or so or until desired thickness, stirring throughout.

When finished, add in herbs if you want, and pour directly into a small glass storage container with a lid as it keeps well and can be stored for future use. Enjoy as a drizzle over organ meat, fresh fruit or various salads.

+ **SIDE NOTE:** Be careful not to boil for long over extreme heat or you will burn the liquid!

MARVELOUS MAYONNAISE

This mayonnaise is a game changer. For years, we messed around with trying to create a delicious and healthier version of mayo in a large blender, but always seemed to fall short. Something wasn't clicking, as it always ended up on the runny side. A whole new world opened up when we purchased a new immersion hand blender. Try this method and you honestly won't believe your eyes. It will emulsify into a glorious thick and creamy texture right before your eyes. This is the regular creation, but feel free to fancy things up by adding in your favorite herbs and spices. We love adding smoked paprika and yellow curry powder.

MAKES 1¾ CUPS (420 ML)

2 large **eggs**

1 tbsp (15 g) **Dijon mustard**

1 tbsp (15 mL) apple cider vinegar

1 tbsp (15 mL) **lemon juice**

1½ cups olive oil (355 mL) not extra virgin, just regular olive oil

½ tsp sea salt

Add the ingredients into a tall immersion blender cup in the order that they appear. Place the immersion hand blender all the way to the bottom of the cup and begin the blend. Mix for about 20 seconds at the bottom and then slowly work your way up to the top, by raising up the immersion blender until all ingredients form into a thick mayonnaise-like consistency. Remove and scoop out into a airtight glass container. Can store in the fridge for up to 1 week.

SRIRACHA SPIKED HOLLANDAISE SAUCE

We love this Hollandaise sauce over bacon and eggs but smothering your favorite vegetables, such as asparagus, would also be ideal! I decided to spruce things up by kicking it up a notch with a splash of Sriracha sauce. If you wish to go the more plain Jane route, feel free to omit it!

MAKES ¾ CUP (180 ML)

3 **egg yolks**

1 tbsp (15 mL) freshly squeezed **lemon juice**

1 tbsp (15 mL) warm water

¼ tsp sea salt

½ cup (120 mL) melted ghee, cooled to room temperature

¼ tsp cayenne pepper

1 tsp **hot sauce** (we recommend Sriracha)

In a medium measuring cup, combine the egg yolks, lemon juice, warm water and sea salt. Take your immersion hand blender and lower it into the measuring cup. Turn it on and blend for a few seconds and then begin slowly pouring in the cooled melted ghee in a light, steady stream. Once blended to your liking, remove the immersion blender and add in the spices and/or hot sauce, stirring thoroughly. Transfer to a small saucepan and keep warm on the stovetop over low heat. Serve over eggs, vegetables or whatever your heart desires.

RESOURCES

AUTOIMMUNE DISEASE

Autoimmune Paleo
www.autoimmune-paleo.com

Paleo Parents
www.paleoparents.com

Terry Wahls M.D.
www.terrywahls.com

The Paleo Mom
www.thepaleomom.com

FOOD RECIPES

Nom Nom Paleo
www.nomnompaleo.com

Paleo Comfort Foods
www.paleocomfortfoods.com

Primal Palate
www.primalpalate.com

The Clothes Make the Girl
www.theclothesmakethegirl.com

The Domestic Man
www.thedomesticman.com

LIFESTYLE

Balanced Bites
www.balancedbites.com

Everyday Paleo
www.everydaypaleo.com

Mark's Daily Apple
www.marksdailyapple.com

Whole 9
www.whole9life.com

MENTAL HEALTH & SLEEP

Dan's Plan
www.dansplan.com

Evolutionary Psychiatry
www.evolutionarypsychiatry.blogspot.ca

Primal Body, Primal Mind
www.primalbody-primalmind.com

MOVEMENT & MOBILITY

Gymnastics Workout of The Day
www.gymnasticswod.com

Ido Portal
www.idoportal.com

Mobility Workout of The Day
www.mobilitywod.com

MovNat
www.movnat.com

NATURAL LIVING & BEAUTY ADVICE

Real Food Liz (formerly Cave Girl Eats)
www.realfoodliz.com

Wellness Mama
www.wellnessmama.com

The Mommypotamus
www.mommypotamus.com

NATURAL SKINCARE & BEAUTY PRODUCTS

Primal Life Organics
www.primallifeorganics.com

Buffalo Gal Grass-fed Beauty
www.buffalogalgrass-fed.com

Wilderness Family Naturals
www.wildernessfamilynaturals.com

SCIENCE & NUTRITION

Health for the 21st Century
www.chriskresser.com

Perfect Health Diet
www.perfecthealthdiet.com

Revolutionary Solutions to Modern Life
www.robbwolf.com

The Daily Lipid
www.blog.cholesterol-and-health.com

Whole Health Source
www.wholehealthsource.blogspot.ca

SOURCING GOOD FOOD

Eat Wild
www.eatwild.com

Eat Well Guide
www.eatwellguide.org

Local Harvest
www.localharvest.org

STRENGTH, CONDITIONING & COACHING

Catalyst Athletics
www.catalystathletics.com

Strength & Conditioning
www.j-mstrength.com

SUSTAINABILITY

Sustainable Dish
www.sustainabledish.com

Farm-to-Consumer Legal Defense Fund
www.farmtoconsumer.org

CANANDIAN PEEPS EH!

HEALTH BLOGS

Summer Innanen
www.summerinnanen.com

Sarah Ramsden
www.sarahramsden.com

Stumptuous
www.stumptuous.com

ATHLETICS

Caveman Strong
www.cavemanstrong.com

CrossFit Toronto
www.crossfitto.com

StrengthBox
www.strengthbox.ca

The Diary of a Nomadic Athlete
www.treehouseofcyn.wordpress.com

FARM FRESH FOOD

Ontario CSA Directory
www.csafarms.ca

Ontario Farm Fresh
www.ontariofarmfresh.com

Farmer's Markets Canada
www.farmersmarketscanada.ca

Urban Rancher
www.urbanranchergta.com

Phoenix and Arnold Beef
www.phoenixandarnold.com

ONLINE GROCERY GRUB

Caveman Grocer
www.cavemangrocer.com

Healthy Planet
www.healthyplanetcanada.com

Noah's Natural Foods
www.noahsnaturalfoods.ca

Upaya Naturals
www.upayanaturals.com

VITAMINS IN FOOD

*Based on 100g serving

	Vit A	Vit B$_p$	Vit B$_1$	Vit B$_2$	Vit B$_3$	Vit B$_5$	Vit B$_6$	Vit B$_9$	Vit B$_{12}$	Vit C	Vit D	Vit E	Vit K
Ahi Tuna		0.141	0.112	0.105	1.379		0.798		0.979		0.133		
Anchovies		0.155		0.279	1.244	0.182	0.156		0.369		0.113	0.322	0.101
Arugula	0.132							0.243		0.167			0.905
Asparagus			0.135					0.373					0.422
Avocados					0.293	0.220	0.223					0.131	0.175
Bacon		0.238	0.383	0.213	0.723	0.262	0.299						
Beef Brisket		0.235		0.160	0.070	0.134	0.252		0.950				
Bella Mushroom					0.391	0.252							
Bibb Lettuce	0.184							0.183					0.853
Bok Choy	0.236						0.128	0.103		0.289			0.283
Broccoli						0.123	0.154	0.270		0.721			1.176
Brussels Sprouts							0.137	0.150		0.689			1.169
Canned Tuna	0.841				0.659		0.400		4.500				
Capers				0.107									0.205
Caraway Seeds		0.230									0.320		
Cashews		0.111	0.157	0.154		0.243	0.197	0.173					0.289
Chicken Breasts					0.347								
Chicken Eggs		0.577		0.380		0.330			0.400		0.147		
Chicken Hearts				0.570	0.175	0.531	0.246	0.200	3.038				
Chicken Livers	4.773	0.594	0.243	1.779	0.870	1.663	0.646	1.400	8.804				
Chicken Wings				0.228	0.444			0.389	0.200				
Chili Powder	1.648			0.720	0.725		1.611					2.542	0.881
Chorizo		0.178	0.521	0.231	0.321	0.224	0.408		0.833		0.100		
Cilantro	0.374									0.300			2.500
Clams			0.125	0.328	0.210	0.136			41.204	0.246			
Cocao				0.185	0.137								
Cod		0.152			0.157		0.218		0.438				
Collard Greens	0.639							0.190		0.293			5.193
Crab Meat							0.138	0.128	4.792				
Cumin Seeds				0.252			0.335					0.222	

	Vit A	Vit B$_p$	Vit B$_1$	Vit B$_2$	Vit B$_3$	Vit B$_5$	Vit B$_6$	Vit B$_9$	Vit B$_{12}$	Vit C	Vit D	Vit E	Vit K
Curry Powder			0.211	0.216	0.217	0.885		0.365				1.466	0.832
Dates					0.101	0.161	0.192						
Dried Figs													0.130
Duck Breast			0.145	0.207	0.302		0.138		0.125				
Duck Eggs	0.216	0.479	0.130	0.311		0.372			2.250		0.113		
Endive	0.120					0.180		0.355					1.925
Fresh Basil	0.923									0.200			3.457
Fresh Dill	0.400					0.370		0.370		0.900			
Fresh Mint	0.226			0.135			0.122	0.263		0.148			
Fresh Rosemary							0.258	0.273		0.252			
Fresh Thyme				0.362			0.268			1.779			
Garlic (Raw)							0.950			0.347			
Gr. Cabbage										0.344			0.573
Ground Almonds				0.744	0.322							1.870	
Ground Beef		0.191		0.238	0.282	0.214	0.307		2.229				
Ground Bison		0.177	0.116	0.203	0.373		0.308		1.017				
Ground Cinnamon							0.122					0.155	0.260
Ground Ginger							0.482						
Ground Lamb		0.235			0.372				1.138				
Ground Nutmeg			0.288				0.123	0.190					
Ground Paprika	2.737		0.275	0.946	0.390	0.502	1.647	0.133				1.989	0.669
Ground Pepper						0.280							1.364
Ground Veal		0.173		0.208	0.502		0.300		0.529				
Halibut		0.137			0.494		0.486		0.529		0.387		
Hazelnuts			0.396			0.163	0.450	0.195				1.167	
Kale	0.817									0.280			7.350
Kelp								0.450					
Lamb Chops		0.197		0.215	0.428	0.132	0.123		1.050				
Lobster		0.147			0.114	0.333			0.596				
Mahi Mahi					0.464	0.173	0.355		0.288				
Mussels			0.250	0.323					10.000				
Mustard												0.957	0.502

	Vit A	Vit B$_p$	Vit B$_1$	Vit B$_2$	Vit B$_3$	Vit B$_5$	Vit B$_6$	Vit B$_9$	Vit B$_{12}$	Vit C	Vit D	Vit E	Vit K
Olive Oil													
Oysters		0.236		0.138	0.116				7.292			0.113	
Parsnips						0.118		0.145		1.444			
Pecans			0.550										
Pine Nuts		0.101	0.303	0.175	0.274							0.622	0.449
Pistachios			0.579			0.513	0.863						
Pork Belly				0.145		0.113			0.200				
Pork Ribs		0.143	0.383	0.255	0.477	0.252	0.318		0.308				
Pork Shoulder		0.198		0.298	0.246	0.273	0.300		0.370				
Raisins				0.147			0.248						
Red Cabbage							0.610			0.663			0.318
Saffron				0.205			0.777	0.233		0.898			
Sardines		0.138		0.179	0.263	0.516			3.750		0.320		
Sea Bass					0.160	0.173	0.266		1.838				
Sea Scallops		0.210							0.896				
Sesame Seeds			0.659	0.190	0.282		0.608	0.243					
Shrimp		0.256							0.692				
Sole		0.145							0.546		0.233		
Spinach	0.521							0.485		0.300			4.024
Squid				0.352	0.163	0.102			0.513				
Sunflower Seeds				0.125	0.422	0.233	0.423	0.593				1.526	
Sweet Potatoes	0.874					0.116	0.127				0.142		
Taro Root				0.152						0.422			
Trout			0.355	0.325	0.361	0.448	0.178		3.121				
Turkey Breast		0.153		0.101	0.468	0.142	0.431		0.163				
Venison			0.208	0.385	0.525	0.181	0.546		0.946				
Walnuts				0.100		0.332	0.448					0.120	
White Potatoes			0.102		0.192	0.171	0.472			0.150			
Wild Salmon		0.205			0.274		0.533		2.363		0.873		

MINERALS IN FOOD
*Based on 100g serving

	Calcium	Copper	Iron	Magnesium	Manganese	Phosphorus	Potassium	Selenium	Zinc
Ahi Tuna			0.115	0.105		0.476	0.112	1.967	
Anchovies	0.232	0.377	0.579	0.173		0.360	0.116		0.222
Arugula	0.160		0.183	0.118	0.140				
Asparagus								0.111	
Avocados		0.189					0.108		
Bacon						0.801		1.182	0.331
Beef Brisket		0.124	0.359			0.306		0.713	0.762
Bella Mushroom		0.432				0.193		0.398	
Bibb Lettuce			0.155						
Bok Choy									
Broccoli									
Brussels Sprouts									
Canned Tuna						0.466		1.462	
Capers		0.416	0.209						
Caraway Seeds									
Cashews		2.467	0.750	0.650	0.359	0.700	0.120	0.213	0.509
Chicken Breasts		0.259				0.300		0.447	
Chicken Eggs			0.236			0.300		0.600	
Chicken Hearts		0.558	1.129			0.284		0.145	0.664
Chicken Livers		0.594	1.610			0.631		0.1204	0.365
Chicken Wings			0.343					0.758	
Chili Powder	0.330	1.111	2.163	0.373	0.739	0.429	0.400	0.370	0.391
Chorizo			0.199			0.214		0.384	0.310
Cilantro		0.250	0.220						
Clams		0.764	3.495	0.435		0.483	0.134	0.154	0.248
Cocao	0.128	4.209	1.733	1.248	1.668	1.049	0.324	0.260	0.619
Cod				0.105		0.197		0.684	
Collard Greens	0.210		0.140						
Crab Meat		1.313		0.158		0.400		0.727	0.693
Cumin Seeds	0.931	0.963	8.295	0.915	1.4444	0.713	0.380		0.436

	Calcium	Copper	Iron	Magnesium	Manganese	Phosphorus	Potassium	Selenium	Zinc
Curry Powder	0.478	0.906	3.669	0.637	1.865	0.449	0.328	0.311	0.368
Dates		0.402	0.113	0.135	0.129				
Dried Figs	0.162	0.319	0.254	0.17	0.222		0.145		
Duck		0.252	0.338			0.223		0.364	0.169
Duck Eggs			0.481			0.314		0.662	0.128
Endive		0.110	0.104		0.183				
Fresh Basil		0.428	0.396		0.499				
Fresh Dill									
Fresh Mint	0.199	0.267	1.484	0.158	0.486				
Fresh Rosemary	0.317	0.334	0.831	0.228	0.417				
Fresh Thyme	0.405	0.617	2.181	0.400	0.747				
Garlic (Raw)	0.181	0.332	0.213		0.727	0.219		0.258	
Gr. Cabbage									
Ground Almonds	0.267	1.233	0.479	0.703	1.006	0.672	0.151		0.300
Ground Beef		0.126	0.384			0.326		0.587	0.898
Ground Bison		0.168	0.399			0.304		0.565	0.485
Ground Cinnamon	1.002	0.377	1.040	0.150	7.594				0.166
Ground Ginger		0.533	2.475	0.535	14.478	0.240	0.280	1.015	0.330
Ground Lamb			0.350			0.290		0.690	0.598
Ground Nutmeg	0.184	1.140	0.380	0.458	1.261	0.304			0.195
Ground Paprika	0.229	0.792	2.643	0.445	0.691	0.449	0.485	0.115	0.394
Ground Pepper	0.443	1.780	1.214	0.428	5.545				
Ground Veal		0.114	0.124			0.310		0.250	-0.352
Halibut						0.410		1.007	
Hazelnuts	0.149	1.778	0.413	0.400	5.500	0.443	0.140		0.200
Kale	0.138		0.118		0.197				
Kelp			0.356	0.300					
Lamb Chops		0.161	0.250			0.323		0.596	0.375
Lobster		1.722		0.108		0.264		1.329	0.268
Mahi Mahi			0.181			0.261	0.113	0.815	
Mussels			0.840		2.957	0.407		1.629	0.243
Mustard								0.598	

	Calcium	Copper	Iron	Magnesium	Manganese	Phosphorus	Potassium	Selenium	Zinc
Olive Oil									
Oysters	0.116	6.341	1.151		0.257	0.277		0.718	7.145
Parsnips		0.153			0.128				
Pecans		1.333	0.316	0.300	1.957				
Pine Nuts		1.471	0.691	3.827		0.821	0.127		0.586
Pistachios		1.432	0.500	0.273	0.540	0.670			
Pork Belly		0.266	0.154			0.184		0.733	0.265
Pork Ribs		0.119	0.115			0.236		0.585	0.279
Pork Shoulder			0.231			0.310		0.818	0.400
Raisins		0.363	0.224		0.134	0.164	0.159		
Red Cabbage			0.100		0.106				
Saffron		0.364	1.388	0.660	12.351	0.360	0.367		
Sardines	0.340	0.302	0.280			0.523		0.738	0.127
Sea Bass			0.135	0.128		0.363		0.851	
Sea Scallops						0.699		0.395	0.141
Sesame Seeds	0.975	4.536	1.819	0.878	1.070	0.899	0.100	0.625	0.705
Shrimp		0.287				0.437		0.900	
Sole						0.441		0.593	
Spinach			0.339		0.390				
Squid		2.349	0.126			0.359		0.942	0.158
Sunflower Seeds		1.770	0.515	0.778	0.901	0.910	0.123	1.878	0.445
Sweet Potatoes		0.104			0.116				
Taro Root	0.149		0.195	0.128			0.133		
Trout		0.268	0.240	0.474		0.449		0.295	
Turkey Breast			0.191			0.382		0.584	0.158
Venison		0.300	0.529			0.389		0.205	0.334
Walnuts		1.511	0.390	0.503	1.694	0.733	0.111	0.309	0.306
White Potatoes		0.908	0.880	0.108	0.268	0.144	0.122		
Wild Salmon						0.453		0.664	

ACKNOWLEDGMENTS

I am so grateful that I reconnected with my good friend from University, Tyler Touchette. You introduced me to the paleo lifestyle, working out and thinking more critically—tough love. I like that. I'm eternally grateful for all you have done, as you set me on the road to better health.

I am so appreciative for the aid I have received with my www.PALEOdISH.com website. John Vivian, co-owner of CrossFit Toronto, your encouragement and assistance was so helpful. You're a computer genius and I have learned a lot from you. I'm super appreciative for that start-up.

I am so thankful I went to my first Paleo Nutrition Workshop back in 2009. Robb Wolf, your down-to-earth, humorous intelligence was definitely a hook for me. Inventor of the Norcal Margarita, I admire your passion and gusto. I'm extremely thankful for your ongoing support.

I am so grateful that I sat down and interviewed biochemist Mat Lalonde PhD in Toronto in 2010. Your brain fascinates me. Dustin and I cherish all our times spent in Boston together. The Kraken. I respect your tell-it-like-it-is way. I'm beyond grateful for your friendship and your patience during this book writing process.

I am so appreciative that this lovely lady helped plant the seed for this book. Diana Rodgers, your gentle nudge and belief in me were the "take me under your wing" feeling that I needed. You're an incredible sustainable farmer and I love that you grow your own food. I'm really appreciative that we have become pals.

I am so thankful that our paths have crossed with people like Michelle Tam & Henry Fong and Julie & Charles Mayfield. That dinner we spent with y'all (trying to sound Southern) in your home in Atlanta was where chatter of this book began. Tip top friends. We love every time we get to see you. I'm very thankful for our bond.

I am so grateful I got to meet this gal in real life last summer. Liz Wolfe, you are the definition of beauty—inside and out. You're an incredible teacher. You have taught me more about self-love than you will ever know. I'm tremendously grateful for your words of wisdom, my sweet sardine sista!

I am so appreciative that I got to work with this unbelievable team. Will, Meg P., Meg B. and Marissa of Page Street Publishing, you all helped me so much. You're an amazing group of people. I'm sincerely appreciative of your flexibility and accommodating ways.

Our families and friends. We're so thankful for each and every one of you. Your support in letting us be who we are is valued. Love to all of you always. A special shout-out to Hayley and Eamon and Joe and Joanne (in-laws) for letting us take over their kitchens to shoot the photographs for this book with the talented Ken Goodman. Ken, you made this book come alive! Also, to Christina for all your help in the kitchen. Big thanks to my family for your encouragement from afar. Lastly to Pheonix and Arnold Farms for supplying the beef during our photoshoot. We are so fortunate to know all of you. Thank you to all our taste-tester friends and Richard and the crew at our favorite local establishment!

ABOUT THE AUTHOR

Cindy Sexton is a small town gal at heart turned semi-city-slicker. She is currently a certified teacher in the Greater Toronto Area who adores all things fitness, food and nutrition related. She is passionate about teaching, as well as learning from others in this field, and is constantly striving toward being a little bit better every single day.

Her laid-back approach to eating "really real" (nutrient-dense) food is reasonable and realistic. With a multi-faceted approach that focuses on returning to the simpler days of living, she concentrates on making play, laughter, sleep and self-care a priority, which makes up her relaxed paleo lifestyle.

If you are looking for her, you will often find her strolling a farmers market, chilling with friends and family, trying new restaurants with her husband, whipping up something in the kitchen or hanging out at the gym. She loves to read (mostly nonfiction), walks on the beach (no joke) and collecting socks (she has a top drawer to prove it). Future endeavors include trying to improve school snack programs and building stronger farm to school partnerships.

Mathieu Lalonde is an organic chemist with a genuine interest in human metabolism, nutritional biochemistry, health and athletic performance. Mat obtained a bachelor's of science in chemistry from the University of Ottawa preceding his departure to Cambridge, Massachusetts, where he attended Harvard University for a doctorate in organic chemistry. Upon the completion of his PhD, Mat reconnected with his lifelong interest in nutrition and decided to apply the rigors of the core sciences to the primary literature published on nutrition. Mat aims to teach individuals how to 1) interpret published material such that they themselves can distinguish between legitimate versus unsound research and 2) evaluate both the strengths and relevancies of publications' reported conclusions. Mat has recently developed an interest in nutrient density and is currently studying both chemical biology and nutritional biochemistry while fulfilling a lecturer position at Harvard.

INDEX

A

Acorn Squash, Pork and Cranberry Stuffed, 131
Akuri Scrambled Eggs, 121
almonds
  nutrients in, 30
  Roasted Broccoli with Garlic and Anchovies, Topped with Toasted Almonds, 174
  Shake 'n' Bake Chops, 30
anchovies
  Lemon-Olive Anchovy Dressing, 201
  Roasted Broccoli with Garlic and Anchovies, Topped with Toasted Almonds, 174
anxiety, 9, 10
apples
  Apple and Cabbage Coleslaw with Dried Tart Cherries, 71
  Really Red Waldorf Salad, 184
  Roasted Turkey Breast with Apple-Orange-Cranberry Sauce, 164
apricots: Lamb Tagine, 180
artichokes
  Roasted Garlic Jerusalem Artichokes with Hazelnuts, 45
  Shaved Roast Beef Salad with Marinated Artichoke Hearts, 95
asparagus
  Prosciutto and Fig Chicken Roll-Ups, 134
  Rosemary and Lamb Potato Pie, 130
  Salmon, Eggs and Asparagus over Buttery Bibb Lettuce, 77
avocado
  Crab Meat with Juicy Mango-Avocado Salsa, 167
  Creamy Avocado-Lime Dressing, 202
  Creamy Garlicky Guacamole, 197
  Mixed Avocado, Bacon and Chicken Bowl, 140
  Santa Fe Omelet with Sliced Avocado, 179
  Sautéed Endive with Shrimp and Ruby Red Grapefruit, 91

B

bacon
  Bacon 'n' Dill Sweet Potato Salad, 133
  Bacon-Crusted Chicken Strips, 61
  Bacon-Wrapped Rosemary Sweet Potato Fries, 22
  Beet and Brussels Sprout Salad, 128
  Eggs Benedict with Potato Latkes, 185–186
  Mixed Avocado, Bacon and Chicken Bowl, 140
  Not-So Boring Meatloaf, 119
  Pan-Seared Scallops with Bacon and Spinach, 143
  Twice-Baked Stuffed Sweet Potato, 178
Baked Sage and Prosciutto Veal Meatballs, 156
balsamic vinegar
  Balsamic and Fig Pork Tenderloin, 85
  Balsamic Reduction, 206
  Classic Sexton Balsamic Vinaigrette, 198
  Five Spice Beef Tenderloin with Thyme Balsamic Mushrooms, 54
  Gingered Balsamic and Date Glazed Chicken Legs, 29
  Sun-Dried Tomato and Basil Vinaigrette, 202
beef
  Burgundy Braised Beef Cheeks, 114
  Chunky Beef Chili, 127
  Citrus Flank Steak over Mixed Greens, 113
  Double-Decker Nachos, 100
  Elvis Burger, 152
  Espresso and Cacao Rubbed Roast Beef Au Jus, 183
  Five Spice Beef Tenderloin with Thyme Balsamic Mushrooms, 54
  Mexican Beef Bowl with Cocao, 151
  Not-So Boring Meatloaf, 119
  Mushroom and Sausage Beef Roll, 81
  Shaved Roast Beef Salad with Marinated Artichoke Hearts, 95
  Shredded Beef Tongue, 107
  Slow-Cooker Cabbage and Beef Casserole, 169
  Spicy Beef Stir Fry with Kelp Noodles, 122
  Spicy Braised Oxtail, 168
  Strip Loin Steak with Roasted Garlic and Rosemary Bone Marrow Butter, 103
  Traditional Newfoundland Jiggs Dinner, 160
beets
  Beet and Brussels Sprout Salad, 128
  Really Red Waldorf Salad, 184
  Root Vegetable Chips with Coarse Sea Salt, 50
bell peppers. See peppers
Bison Burgers, Inside-Out, 191
Black Pepper Seared Ahi Tuna Steak with Pickled Ginger, 49
bok choy
  Green Curried Butternut Squash Skillet, 175
  Thai Chicken and Kelp Noodle Soup, 146
bone marrow: Strip Loin Steak with Roasted Garlic and Rosemary Bone Marrow Butter, 103
Broccoli with Garlic and Anchovies, Topped with Toasted Almonds, Roasted, 174
Brussels Sprout Salad, Beet and, 128

burgers
Elvis Burger, 152
Inside-Out Bison Burgers, 191
Moroccan Lamb Burgers, 177
Burgundy Braised Beef Cheeks, 114
butternut squash
Creamy Roasted Butternut Squash
Soup with Ginger & Cilantro, 26
Green Curried Butternut Squash
Skillet, 175
Buttery Lamb Chops Infused with Mint
and Lemon, 82

C
cabbage
Apple and Cabbage Coleslaw with
Dried Tart Cherries, 71
Duck Fat Cabbage with Pork &
Caraway Seeds, 65
Slow-Cooker Cabbage and Beef
Casserole, 169
Traditional Newfoundland Jiggs
Dinner, 160
cacao: Espresso and Cacao Rubbed
Roast Beef Au Jus, 183
calcium, 13
capers
Lemon Caper Oven Baked Trout with
Fresh Dill and Browned Butter, 188
nutrients in, 155
Spicy Stuffed Roasted Bell
Peppers, 155
caraway seeds, 65
carrots
Parsnip and Carrot Mash with a
Hint of Nutmeg, 31
Rosemary and Lamb Potato Pie, 130
Traditional Newfoundland Jiggs
Dinner, 160
cashews, 110
cassava: Root Vegetable Chips with
Coarse Sea Salt, 50
cauliflower
Orange-Infused Kale Salad with
Cauliflower "Couscous", 159
Roasted Cauliflower with Raisins
and Pine Nuts, 106
Spicy Stuffed Roasted Bell
Peppers, 155
celery root: Velvety Roasted Parsnip
and Celery Root Soup with Crumbled
Pancetta, 141
cherries
Apple and Cabbage Coleslaw with
Dried Tart Cherries, 71

Roasted Duck Breast with Gingered
Cherry Sauce, 88
chicken
Bacon-Crusted Chicken Strips, 61
Chicken Heart Skewers with
Chimichurri Sauce, 98
Gingered Balsamic and Date Glazed
Chicken Legs, 29
Herb Buttered Whole Chicken
Stuffed with Sauerkraut, 117
Indian Butter Chicken, 110
Marinated and Baked Chicken
Thighs--3 Ways, 68–70
Mixed Avocado, Bacon and Chicken
Bowl, 140
Pan-Fried Chicken Livers with Pork
Lardons, 67
Prosciutto and Fig Chicken
Roll-Ups, 134
Really Red Waldorf Salad, 184
Thai Chicken and Kelp Noodle
Soup, 146
Tomato Braised Chicken Dish, 48
Zesty Lime Sriracha Wings, 25
Chili, Chunky Beef, 127
Chimichurri Sauce, 98
chocolate: Mexican Beef Bowl with
Cocao, 151
choline, 12
chorizo
Chorizo and Kale with Sautéed
Onions, 36
Sweet Potato and Yam Crusted
Spinach and Chorizo Quiche, 73
Chunky Beef Chili, 127
Cider Collard Greens with Pancetta, 32
Citrus Flank Steak over Mixed
Greens, 113
clams
Clam Curried Mussels, 35
Littleneck Clams with Shallot
and Garlic Butter, 99
Classic Sexton Balsamic Vinaigrette, 198
Cobb Salad with Bay Scallops, 170
coconut
Creamy Coconut-Mustard Dressing,
205
Green Curried Butternut Squash
Skillet, 175
Cod, Pan-Fried Basil Pesto, 39
Coleslaw with Dried Tart Cherries,
Apple and Cabbage, 71
Collard Greens with Pancetta, Cider, 32
common sense, 10
cooking, passion for, 19

cooking fats, 16
copper, 13
Cornish Hens, Tandoori, 57
Crab Meat with Juicy Mango-Avocado
Salsa, 167
cranberries
Pork and Cranberry Stuffed Acorn
Squash, 131
Roasted Turkey Breast with Apple-
Orange-Cranberry Sauce, 164
Creamy Avocado-Lime Dressing, 202
Creamy Coconut-Mustard Dressing, 205
Creamy Garlicky Guacamole, 197
Creamy Roasted Butternut Squash
Soup with Ginger & Cilantro, 26
cucumbers: Oysters with
Mignonettes—3 Ways, 92
cumin seeds, 62
Curried Egg Salad, 94

D
dates: Gingered Balsamic and Date
Glazed Chicken Legs, 29
dieting, 9
digestive problems, 9, 10
Dilly Tuna Salad, 120
dips, dressings, and sauces
Apple-Orange-Cranberry Sauce, 164
Balsamic Reduction, 206
Chimichurri Sauce, 98
Classic Sexton Balsamic Vinaigrette,
198
Creamy Avocado-Lime Dressing, 202
Creamy Coconut-Mustard
Dressing, 205
Creamy Garlicky Guacamole, 197
Hollandaise sauce, 185–186
Honey-Mustard Dressing, 205
Hot 'N' Spicy Salsa, 194
Lemon-Olive Anchovy Dressing, 201
Marvelous Mayonnaise, 206
Orange Citrus Dressing, 198
Sesame Ginger Dressing, 201
Sriracha Spiked Hollandaise
sauce, 207
Sun-Dried Tomato and Basil
Vinaigrette, 202
Double-Decker Nachos, 100
dressings. See dips, dressings, and
sauces
duck
Duck Fat Cabbage with Pork &
Caraway Seeds, 65
Potato and Hungarian Sausage Hash
with Fried Duck Eggs, 144

Roasted Duck Breast with Gingered Cherry Sauce, 88

E

eggs
Akuri Scrambled Eggs, 121
Curried Egg Salad, 94
Eggs Benedict with Potato Latkes, 185–186
Niçoise(ish) Salad with Roasted Fingerlings and Sardines, 173
Potato and Hungarian Sausage Hash with Fried Duck Eggs, 144
Salmon, Eggs and Asparagus over Buttery Bibb Lettuce, 77
Santa Fe Omelet with Sliced Avocado, 179
Elvis Burger, 152
empty calories, 9
Endive with Shrimp and Ruby Red Grapefruit, Sautéed, 91
Espresso and Cacao Rubbed Roast Beef Au Jus, 183

F

fennel: Zucchini, Fennel and Sardines in Marinara Sauce, 84
figs
Balsamic and Fig Pork Tenderloin, 85
Orange-Infused Kale Salad with Cauliflower "Couscous", 159
Prosciutto Fig and Chicken Roll-Ups, 134
fish
See also seafood
Black Pepper Seared Ahi Tuna Steak with Pickled Ginger, 49
Dilly Tuna Salad, 120
Lemon and Tomato Baked Halibut in Parchment Pouches, 148
Lemon Caper Oven Baked Trout with Fresh Dill and Browned Butter, 188
Mahi Mahi Fish Kebab with Grilled Pineapple, 58
Mustard-Crusted Salmon, 66
Niçoise(ish) Salad with Roasted Fingerlings and Sardines, 173
Pan-Fried Basil Pesto Cod, 39
Pan-Fried Sole with Mushroom and Tarragon Sauce, 78
Salmon, Eggs and Asparagus over Buttery Bibb Lettuce, 77
Sauerkraut Salmon Salad, 147
Sesame Crusted Sea Bass with Garlic-Infused Baby Shrimp, 43

Zucchini, Fennel and Sardines in Marinara Sauce, 84
Five Spice Beef Tenderloin with Thyme Balsamic Mushrooms, 54
folate, 12
foods
minerals in, 214–216
nutrient dense, 10–14
real, 9, 15–16
vitamins in, 211–213
fruits. *See specific fruits*

G

garlic
Littleneck Clams with Shallot and Garlic Butter, 99
Pork Belly with Garlic Mashed Potatoes, 40–42
Roasted Broccoli with Garlic and Anchovies, Topped with Toasted Almonds, 174
Roasted Garlic Jerusalem Artichokes with Hazelnuts, 45
Strip Loin Steak with Roasted Garlic and Rosemary Bone Marrow Butter, 103
Warm Mushroom and Garlic Salad with Prosciutto Crisps, 123
ginger
Black Pepper Seared Ahi Tuna Steak with Pickled Ginger, 49
Creamy Roasted Butternut Squash Soup with Ginger & Cilantro, 26
Gingered Balsamic and Date Glazed Chicken Legs, 29
nutrients in, 26
Roasted Duck Breast with Gingered Cherry Sauce, 88
Sesame Ginger Dressing, 201
grains, 11
grapefruit: Sautéed Endive with Shrimp and Ruby Red Grapefruit, 91
grapes: Really Red Waldorf Salad, 184
Green Curried Butternut Squash Skillet, 175
greens
Chorizo and Kale with Sautéed Onions, 36
Cider Collard Greens with Pancetta, 32
Citrus Flank Steak over Mixed Greens, 113
Cobb Salad with Bay Scallops, 170
Shaved Roast Beef Salad with Marinated Artichoke Hearts, 95

grocer ingredients, 18
grocery lists, 19
Guacamole, Creamy Garlicky, 197
gut microbiota, 15

H

Halibut in Parchment Pouches, Lemon and Tomato Baked, 148
ham: Inside-Out Bison Burgers, 191
Hash with Fried Duck Eggs, Potato and Hungarian Sausage, 144
hazelnuts: Roasted Garlic Jerusalem Artichokes with Hazelnuts, 45
healing, 15
health practitioners, 15
Herb Buttered Whole Chicken Stuffed with Sauerkraut, 117
herbs, 17
Hollandaise sauce
Eggs Benedict with Potato Latkes, 185–186
Sriracha Spiked Hollandaise Sauce, 207
Honey-Mustard Dressing, 205
Hot 'N' Spicy Salsa, 194

I

Indian Butter Chicken, 110
ingredients, 16–18
Inside-Out Bison Burgers, 191
instant gratification, 10
iron, 13, 25

J

Juniper Berry and Pomegranate Sauce, Venison with, 97

K

kale
Chorizo and Kale with Sautéed Onions, 36
Orange-Infused Kale Salad with Cauliflower "Couscous", 159
kelp
Spicy Beef Stir Fry with Kelp Noodles, 122
Thai Chicken and Kelp Noodle Soup, 146

L

Lalonde, Mathieu, 10–11
lamb
Buttery Lamb Chops Infused with Mint and Lemon, 82

Lamb Tagine, 180

Moroccan Lamb Burgers, 177

Rosemary and Lamb Potato Pie, 130

legumes, 11

lemon

Buttery Lamb Chops Infused with Mint and Lemon, 82

Lemon and Tomato Baked Halibut in Parchment Pouches, 148

Lemon Caper Oven Baked Trout with Fresh Dill and Browned Butter, 188

Lemon-Olive Anchovy Dressing, 201

lettuce

Salmon, Eggs and Asparagus over Buttery Bibb Lettuce, 77

Littleneck Clams with Shallot and Garlic Butter, 99

lobster

Lobster Bisque, 176

Lobster with Tarragon Parsnip Fries, 46

M

magnesium, 14

Mahi Mahi Fish Kebab with Grilled Pineapple, 58

manganese, 14, 26

Mango-Avocado Salsa, Crab Meat with Juicy, 167

Maple Chipotle Glazed Baby Back Pork Ribs, 87

Marinated and Baked Chicken Thighs—3 Ways, 68–70

Mayonnaise, Marvelous, 206

meal plans, 19

Meatballs, Baked Sage and Prosciutto Veal, 156

Mexican Beef Bowl with Cocoa, 151

minerals, 13–14, 214–216

minimal ingredient recipes, 16

Mixed Avocado, Bacon and Chicken Bowl, 140

money saving tips, 16

Moroccan Lamb Burgers, 177

mushrooms

Five Spice Beef Tenderloin with Thyme Balsamic Mushrooms, 54

Honey-Mustard Dressing, 205

Pan-Fried Sole with Mushroom and Tarragon Sauce, 78

Mushroom and Sausage Beef Roll, 81

Spicy Beef Stir Fry with Kelp Noodles, 122

Warm Mushroom and Garlic Salad with Prosciutto Crisps, 123

mussels

Clam Curried Mussels, 35

Saffron Stuffed Mussels, 118

mustard

Creamy Coconut-Mustard Dressing, 205

Honey-Mustard Dressing, 205

Mustard-Crusted Salmon, 66

N

Nachos, Double-Decker, 100

niacin, 12, 25

Niçoise(ish) Salad with Roasted Fingerlings and Sardines, 173

noodles

Spicy Beef Stir Fry with Kelp Noodles, 122

Thai Chicken and Kelp Noodle Soup, 146

Zucchini Noodles with Sautéed Shrimp, 137

Not-So Boring Meatloaf, 119

nutmeg, 31

nutrient density, 10–14, 18

nuts

Beet and Brussels Sprout Salad, 128

Pear and Prosciutto Salad with Toasted Pine Nuts, 104

Roasted Broccoli with Garlic and Anchovies, Topped with Toasted Almonds, 174

Roasted Cauliflower with Raisins and Pine Nuts, 106

Roasted Garlic Jerusalem Artichokes with Hazelnuts, 45

O

olives

Lemon-Olive Anchovy Dressing, 201

Olive and Sun-Dried Tomato Spaghetti Squash, 137

onions

Chorizo and Kale with Sautéed Onions, 36

Rosemary and Lamb Potato Pie, 130

Sage-Infused Mustard and Onion Pork Chops, 74

orange

Orange Citrus Dressing, 198

Orange-Infused Kale Salad with Cauliflower "Couscous," 159

Roasted Turkey Breast with Apple-Orange-Cranberry Sauce, 164

Oxtail, Spicy Braised, 168

Oysters with Mignonettes—3 Ways, 92

P

pancetta

Cider Collard Greens with Pancetta, 32

Velvety Roasted Parsnip and Celery Root Soup with Crumbled Pancetta, 141

Pan-Fried Basil Pesto Cod, 39

Pan-Fried Chicken Livers with Pork Lardons, 67

Pan-Fried Sole with Mushroom and Tarragon Sauce, 78

panic attacks, 9, 10

Pan-Seared Scallops with Bacon and Spinach, 143

pantothenic acid, 12

pantry items, 16–17

parsnip

Lobster with Tarragon Parsnip Fries, 46

Parsnip and Carrot Mash with a Hint of Nutmeg, 31

Velvety Roasted Parsnip and Celery Root Soup with Crumbled Pancetta, 141

Pear and Prosciutto Salad with Toasted Pine Nuts, 104

peppers

Hot 'N' Spicy Salsa, 194

Poached Squid Salad, 163

Spicy Stuffed Roasted Bell Peppers, 155

Pesto Cod, Pan-Fried Basil, 39

phosphorus, 14, 25

pine nuts

Pear and Prosciutto Salad with Toasted Pine Nuts, 104

Roasted Cauliflower with Raisins and Pine Nuts, 106

pineapple: Mahi Mahi Fish Kebab with Grilled Pineapple, 58

pistachio nuts, 128

plantains: Elvis Burger, 152

Poached Squid Salad, 163

pork

See also bacon; sausage

Balsamic and Fig Pork Tenderloin, 85

Duck Fat Cabbage with Pork & Caraway Seeds, 65

Maple Chipotle Glazed Baby Back Pork Ribs, 87

Not-So Boring Meatloaf, 119

Pan-Fried Chicken Livers with Pork Lardons, 67

Pork and Cranberry Stuffed Acorn Squash, 131

Pork Belly with Garlic Mashed
Potatoes, 40–42
Sage-Infused Mustard and Onion
Pork Chops, 74
Shake 'n' Bake Chops, 30
Slow & Steady Spiced Pork
Shoulder, 62
Spicy Stuffed Roasted Bell
Peppers, 155
potassium, 14
potatoes
Eggs Benedict with Potato Latkes,
185–186
Niçoise(ish) Salad with Roasted
Fingerlings and Sardines, 173
Pork Belly with Garlic Mashed
Potatoes, 40–42
Potato and Hungarian Sausage Hash
with Fried Duck Eggs, 144
poultry
See also chicken
Duck Fat Cabbage with Pork &
Caraway Seeds, 65
Potato and Hungarian Sausage Hash
with Fried Duck Eggs, 144
Roasted Duck Breast with Gingered
Cherry Sauce, 88
Roasted Turkey Breast with Apple-
Orange-Cranberry Sauce, 164
Tandoori Cornish Hens, 57
Twice-Baked Stuffed Sweet
Potato, 178
prosciutto
Baked Sage and Prosciutto Veal
Meatballs, 156
Pear and Prosciutto Salad with
Toasted Pine Nuts, 104
Prosciutto and Fig Chicken
Roll-Ups, 134
Warm Mushroom and Garlic Salad
with Prosciutto Crisps, 123
pyridoxine, 12

Q
Quiche, Sweet Potato and Yam Crusted
Spinach and Chorizo, 73

R
raisins: Roasted Cauliflower with
Raisins and Pine Nuts, 106
real foods
benefits of eating, 9, 15
ways to save money on, 16
Really Red Waldorf Salad, 184
resources, 208–210
riboflavin, 12

Roasted Broccoli with Garlic and
Anchovies, Topped with Toasted
Almonds, 174
Roasted Cauliflower with Raisins and
Pine Nuts, 106
Roasted Duck Breast with Gingered
Cherry Sauce, 88
Roasted Garlic Jerusalem Artichokes
with Hazelnuts, 45
Roasted Turkey Breast with Apple-
Orange-Cranberry Sauce, 164
Root Vegetable Chips with Coarse
Sea Salt, 50
rosemary
nutrients in, 117
Rosemary and Lamb Potato Pie, 130

S
Saffron Stuffed Mussels, 118
Sage-Infused Mustard and Onion Pork
Chops, 74
salad dressings. See dips, dressings,
and sauces
salads
Bacon 'n' Dill Sweet Potato Salad, 133
Beet and Brussels Sprout Salad, 128
Cobb Salad with Bay Scallops, 170
Dilly Tuna Salad, 120
Niçoise(ish) Salad with Roasted
Fingerlings and Sardines, 173
Orange-Infused Kale Salad with
Cauliflower "Couscous", 159
Pear and Prosciutto Salad with
Toasted Pine Nuts, 104
Poached Squid Salad, 163
Really Red Waldorf Salad, 184
Sauerkraut Salmon Salad, 147
Shaved Roast Beef Salad with
Marinated Artichoke Hearts, 95
Warm Mushroom and Garlic Salad
with Prosciutto Crisps, 123
salmon
Mustard-Crusted Salmon, 66
Salmon, Eggs and Asparagus over
Buttery Bibb Lettuce, 77
Sauerkraut Salmon Salad, 147
Salsa, Hot 'N' Spicy, 194
Santa Fe Omelet with Sliced Avocado,
179
sardines
Niçoise(ish) Salad with Roasted
Fingerlings and Sardines, 173
Zucchini, Fennel and Sardines in
Marinara Sauce, 84
sauces. See dips, dressings, and sauces

sauerkraut
Herb Buttered Whole Chicken
Stuffed with Sauerkraut, 117
Sauerkraut Salmon Salad, 147
sausage
Chorizo and Kale with Sautéed
Onions, 36
Potato and Hungarian Sausage Hash
with Fried Duck Eggs, 144
Mushroom and Sausage Beef Roll, 81
Sweet Potato and Yam Crusted
Spinach and Chorizo Quiche, 73
Sautéed Endive with Shrimp and Ruby
Red Grapefruit, 91
scallops
Cobb Salad with Bay Scallops, 170
Pan-Seared Scallops with Bacon and
Spinach, 143
Sea Bass with Garlic-Infused Baby
Shrimp, Sesame Crusted, 43
seafood
See also fish
Clam Curried Mussels, 35
Cobb Salad with Bay Scallops, 170
Crab Meat with Juicy Mango-
Avocado Salsa, 167
Littleneck Clams with Shallot and
Garlic Butter, 99
Lobster Bisque, 176
Lobster with Tarragon Parsnip Fries,
46
Oysters with Mignonettes—3 Ways,
92
Pan-Seared Scallops with Bacon and
Spinach, 143
Poached Squid Salad, 163
Saffron Stuffed Mussels, 118
Sautéed Endive with Shrimp and
Ruby Red Grapefruit, 91
Zucchini Noodles with Sautéed
Shrimp, 137
selenium, 14
self-care, 14–15
Sesame Crusted Sea Bass with G
arlic-Infused Baby Shrimp, 43
Sesame Ginger Dressing, 201
sesame seeds, 43
Shake 'n' Bake Chops, 30
Shaved Roast Beef Salad with
Marinated Artichoke Hearts, 95
shellfish. See seafood
Shredded Beef Tongue, 107
shrimp
Sautéed Endive with Shrimp and
Ruby Red Grapefruit, 91

Sesame Crusted Sea Bass with Garlic-Infused Baby Shrimp, 43

Zucchini Noodles with Sautéed Shrimp, 137

Slow & Steady Spiced Pork Shoulder, 62

Slow-Cooker Cabbage and Beef Casserole, 169

Sole with Mushroom and Tarragon Sauce, Pan-Fried, 78

soups and stews
Chunky Beef Chili, 127
Clam Curried Mussels, 35
Creamy Roasted Butternut Squash Soup with Ginger & Cilantro, 26
Lobster Bisque, 176
Thai Chicken and Kelp Noodle Soup, 146
Velvety Roasted Parsnip and Celery Root Soup with Crumbled Pancetta, 141

Spaghetti Squash, Olive and Sun-Dried Tomato, 137

spices, 17

Spicy Beef Stir Fry with Kelp Noodles, 122

Spicy Braised Oxtail, 168

Spicy Stuffed Roasted Bell Peppers, 155

spinach
Pan-Seared Scallops with Bacon and Spinach, 143
Sweet Potato and Yam Crusted Spinach and Chorizo Quiche, 73

squash
Creamy Roasted Butternut Squash Soup with Ginger & Cilantro, 26
Green Curried Butternut Squash Skillet, 175
Olive and Sun-Dried Tomato Spaghetti Squash, 137
Pork and Cranberry Stuffed Acorn Squash, 131

Squid Salad, Poached, 163

Sriracha Spiked Hollandaise Sauce, 207

steak. See beef

Strip Loin Steak with Roasted Garlic and Rosemary Bone Marrow Butter, 103

sun-dried tomatoes
Olive and Sun-Dried Tomato Spaghetti Squash, 137
Sun-Dried Tomato and Basil Vinaigrette, 202

sweet potatoes
Bacon 'n' Dill Sweet Potato Salad, 133
Bacon-Wrapped Rosemary Sweet Potato Fries, 22
Rosemary and Lamb Potato Pie, 130

Sweet Potato and Yam Crusted Spinach and Chorizo Quiche, 73

Sweet Potato Aloo Gobi, 124

Twice-Baked Stuffed Sweet Potato, 178

T

Tandoori Cornish Hens, 57

Thai Chicken and Kelp Noodle Soup, 146

thiamine, 12

tomatoes
Hot 'N' Spicy Salsa, 194
Lemon and Tomato Baked Halibut in Parchment Pouches, 148
Olive and Sun-Dried Tomato Spaghetti Squash, 137
Sun-Dried Tomato and Basil Vinaigrette, 202
Tomato Braised Chicken Dish, 48

Touchette, Tyler, 9, 10

Traditional Newfoundland Jiggs Dinner, 160

Trout with Fresh Dill and Browned Butter, Lemon Caper Oven Baked, 188

tuna
Black Pepper Seared Ahi Tuna Steak with Pickled Ginger, 49
Dilly Tuna Salad, 120

turkey
Roasted Turkey Breast with Apple-Orange-Cranberry Sauce, 164
Twice-Baked Stuffed Sweet Potato, 178

Twice-Baked Stuffed Sweet Potato, 178

V

Veal Meatballs, Baked Sage and Prosciutto, 156

vegetables. See specific vegetables

Velvety Roasted Parsnip and Celery Root Soup with Crumbled Pancetta, 141

Venison with Juniper Berry and Pomegranate Sauce, 97

vinaigrette
Balsamic Reduction, 206
Classic Sexton Balsamic Vinaigrette, 198
Sun-Dried Tomato and Basil Vinaigrette, 202

vinegars, 17

vitamin A, 12

vitamin B_1 thiamine, 12

vitamin B_{12}, 13

vitamin B_2 (riboflavin), 12

vitamin B_3 (niacin), 12

vitamin B_5 (pantothenic acid), 12

vitamin B_6 (pyridoxine), 12

vitamin B_9 (folate), 12

vitamin B_p (choline), 12

vitamin C, 13

vitamin D, 13

vitamin E, 13

vitamin K, 13

vitamins, 12–13, 211–213

W

Warm Mushroom and Garlic Salad with Prosciutto Crisps, 123

weight loss, 9

whole foods, 10

Y

yams
Root Vegetable Chips with Coarse Sea Salt, 50
Sweet Potato and Yam Crusted Spinach and Chorizo Quiche, 73

yuca root: Root Vegetable Chips with Coarse Sea Salt, 50

Z

Zesty Lime Sriracha Wings, 25

zinc, 14

zucchini
Zucchini, Fennel and Sardines in Marinara Sauce, 84
Zucchini Noodles with Sautéed Shrimp, 137